THE BRITISH CRUISE SHIP

THE BRITISH CRUISE SHIP

An Illustrated History 1844–1939

Ian Collard

AMBERLEY

First published 2013

Amberley Publishing
The Hill, Stroud
Gloucestershire, GL5 4EP

www.amberley-books.com

British Library Cataloguing in Publication Data.
A catalogue record for this book is available from the British Library.

ISBN 978 1 4456 2121 0
E-Book ISBN: 978-1-4456-2130-2

Typeset in 10pt on 12pt Celeste OT.
Typesetting and Origination by Amberley Publishing.
Printed and bound in the UK by CPI Colour.

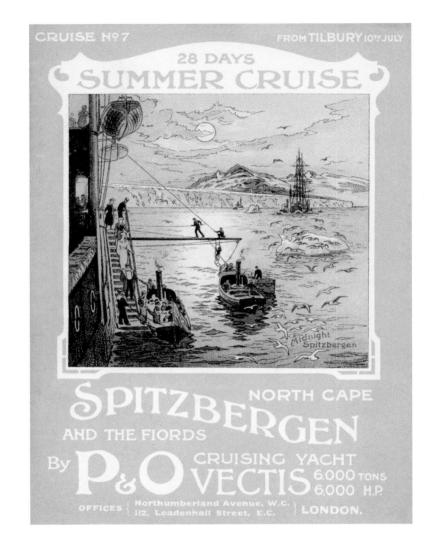

INTRODUCTION

In the nineteenth and early twentieth centuries a cruise ship was described as a passenger vessel used for pleasure voyages. This was in contrast to the normal line voyage of a ship where passengers were transported to another port or country. Cruises normally start and terminate at a particular port and are usually in a region or continent. From the early twentieth century, cruises were operated by passenger liners, which were taken off their normal routes to provide the service and then returned to their regular line voyages. However, some ships were designed and built as cruise liners and were employed around the year providing this service.

Ocean liners differed in several respects to cruise vessels, as they were designed to transport passengers and cargo on long voyages, which required them to be built to a higher standard. Their deep draught prevented them from entering some ports and their enclosed decks were unsuitable for warmer climates, where passengers wished to enjoy the warm fresh air and the sunshine. They were built to deal with the winter North Atlantic weather and because of this their fuel consumption was normally very high.

The steamer *St Andrew* took passengers on an excursion from Glasgow in 1827 to Londonderry, Tobermory, Fort William and Campbeltown offering overnight accommodation at each port. It has been claimed that *Francesco I* was the first cruise ship, as in 1833 she sailed from Naples with nobility from all over Europe. The three-month cruise took her to Taormina, Catania, Syracuse, Malta, Corfu, Patras, Delphi, Zante, Athens, Smyrna and Constantinople, and offered excursions and guided tours at each port of call.

It was as early as 1844 when P&O came up with the idea of offering deep-sea cruising to the Mediterranean. Passengers would travel on their steamers to Malta, Athens, Smyrna, Constantinople, Rhodes, Jaffa and Egypt, and then return back to England. Shore excursions were offered at each port. In 1835, Arthur Anderson placed some dummy advertisements in the Shetland Journal to encourage tourists to travel to the Shetland Islands. The North of Scotland & Orkney & Shetland Steam Navigation Company offered cruises between Scotland and Norway in 1886 by the *St Rognvald* and later, the *St Sunniva* at £10 per person.

P&O's *Ceylon* was sold to John L. Clark in 1881 and was claimed to be the first ship to cruise around the world. She was chartered to the Polytechnic

Touring Association in 1892, owned by Ocean Steam Yachting Company Limited, and survived until 1907 when she was demolished. The Wilson Line offered cruises from Hull to the North Cape, the Norwegian fjords and the Mediterranean in the winter months by the *Domino*, *Angelo* and *Eldorado*.

M. Langlands & Sons introduced coastal cruises from Liverpool and Ardrossan to the Western Isles by the steamer *Princess Royal*. *Princess Victoria* was built in 1894 to provide West Highland cruises, and Orme Brothers & Company operated *Dunara Castle* from 1875; later John McCallum & Company offered cruises by *Hebridean* and *Hebrides*.

Salvesen were responsible for a programme of cruises to Norway and the Baltic in 1887, as were Currie's Castle Line and the Union Steamship Company in the same year. The Orient Line followed in 1889 by advertising cruises to Norway and the Mediterranean by their steamers *Chimborazo* and *Garonne*. In 1895 *Lusitania* made a sixty-day cruise from London Madeira, Tenerife, the Azores and the West Indies. The *Ophir* of 1891 was employed on cruising duties. Her luxury made her popular with passengers and she was considered the 'Queen' of the Indian Ocean. She was very successful and was chartered to become the royal yacht in 1901, for the visit of the Duke and Duchess of Kent (later HM King George V and *Queen Mary*) to Australia.

The North of Scotland & Orkney & Shetland Steam Navigation and the Orient Line were taken over by P&O and the *Rome* was converted to cruising in 1903 and renamed *Vectis*. She carried 187 first- and 46 second-class passengers as *Rome*, but only 160 first class when cruising as *Vectis*. In 1913, *Caledonia* and *Mantua* were employed in cruising to the Norwegian fjords and *Midnight Sun* operated from Newcastle. *Midnight Sun* was originally the German liner *General Werder* and was operated by Armstrong, Mitchell & Company to provide cruises to the Norwegian fjords from Newcastle for up to 700 passengers.

The German Hamburg America Line's *Augusta Victoria* was employed on a Mediterranean cruise from 22 January to 22 March 1891, carrying 241 passengers, including the general manager Albert Ballin and his wife. *Augusta Victoria* was later converted and upgraded to carry passengers on cruises to the West Indies, Norway and the Far East. She was replaced by the new *Prinzessin Victoria Luise* in 1901, and cruised to the Mediterranean, West Indies, Black Sea and Norway. When she was wrecked in 1907, she was replaced by the *Scot*, becoming *Oceana*. Unfortunately, her fuel consumption was very high and she was replaced by *Deutschland* in 1911 and renamed *Victoria Luise*.

The Royal Mail Line steamer *La Plata* offered cruises in 1901, and after 1905 they provided West Indies cruises for passengers disembarking from their South American steamers and cruising in the Caribbean on the *Solent* and the *Berbice*. *Amazon* and *Avon* were employed on Norwegian fjord and Northern Capital cruises. *Ortona* was converted into a cruise liner in 1912 and renamed *Arcadian*. The Royal Mail Steam Packet Company was formed in 1839 by James MacQueen and was incorporated under a royal charter on 26 September that year. MacQueen was known as a businessman, traveller and journalist, and the company was founded on the improvement of the overseas mail service. The original fleet was built to carry passengers and mail, and was described by MacQueen as 'ocean stage coaches'. The vessels in the fleet were mainly passenger/cargo ships, but as the Admiralty granted the mail contract they insisted that they had a strong influence in the construction of the vessels.

Amazon and *Avon* were ideal steamers to introduce the idea of cruising. They were the first vessels in the fleet to provide deluxe suites with bedsteads, single-berth cabins, electric fans and various other innovations. The saloons and public rooms were decorated in the manner of Grinling Gibbons, Adam and other interior decorators of the time. The entrance hall was panelled in carved oak with wide stairways and high deckheads.

Aragon sailed on her maiden voyage from Southampton on 14 July 1905 and was followed by *Amazon*, *Araguaya*, *Avon* and *Asturias*. They were so successful that further passenger tonnage was laid down, and by 1915 *Arlanza*, *Andes*, *Alcantara* and *Almanzora* had been completed by Harland & Wolff. *Dunottar Castle* was chartered to the travel agent Sir Henry Lunn Limited in 1909 and was employed on a cruising schedule. She was purchased by the Royal Mail Lines in 1913 and renamed *Caribbean*. The success of ocean cruising enabled Royal Mail Lines to refit the *Atlantis*, originally the *Andes*, in 1930 and she proved a popular ship with cruise passengers.

In 1906, Cunard's *Caronia* cruised from New York to the Mediterranean. In 1839 Samuel Cunard was introduced to Robert Napier, an experienced engineer, and George Burns and David MacIver, shipowners in the British coastal trade, and a contract was signed between the Lords of the Admiralty to provide a transatlantic mail service. The departure of the wooden paddle steamer *Britannia* from Liverpool on 4 July 1840 marked the beginning of a great adventure by Cunard, who had arrived in England from Canada in 1839. He and his brothers had been involved in various shipping operations, including managing the agency for the East India Company. *Britannia* took fourteen days, eight hours to reach New York on her maiden voyage.

The beginning of the twentieth century saw Cunard looking at new ideas of machinery and propulsion. *Caronia* was introduced in 1905 with quadruple expansion engines and *Carmania* was installed with high-powered steam turbines that made her 1½ knots faster than her sister ship. The turbines developed over 18,000 hp giving her a speed of 21 knots on trails, enabling Cunard to consider this type of propulsion for two vessels *Mauretania* and *Lusitania*, which were being planned at this time.

These two vessels were to be the largest and fastest of their type, and on her second voyage in 1907 *Lusitania* took the Blue Riband record with an average speed of 24 knots. *Mauretania* followed her into service and on her return homeward maiden voyage she beat *Lusitania*'s time by twenty-one minutes by completing the voyage in four days, twenty-two hours and twenty-nine minutes. *Mauretania* became one of Cunard Line's most famous ships, and for more than twenty-two years she was the fastest liner on the North Atlantic. For twenty-seven consecutive voyages she averaged a speed of 25½ knots.

The Boston route saw the commissioning of *Franconia* in 1911 and *Laconia* in 1912, which were Cunard's first dual-purpose cruise vessels. The Thompson Line was purchased to strengthen the Canadian routes, and Anchor Line (Henderson Brothers) was taken over. *Franconia*'s maiden voyage was from New York to the Mediterranean, and her sister *Laconia* was also employed in cruising duties when she sailed on her maiden voyage one year later. Both vessels were employed on the Liverpool–Boston routes and in winter they replaced the *Ultonia* on the New York–Trieste service.

The interwar years brought about a better choice of routes and ships for those wishing to plan an ocean cruise. The shipping lines saw the opportunity to increase revenue and to have their vessels employed for most of the year. Many companies operated their line voyages throughout the busy summer months and sent their ships on cruising duties during the winter. Christmas provided a short season, and special arrangements were made to make the ship more at home than usual. Christmas trees, festive decorations, Santa Claus, puddings and seasonable fare and even a visit to the refrigeration plant to provide some snow. The Christmas cruises at this time normally included New Year and the celebrations associated with Hogmanay. As part of the fleet replacement programme, Cunard took delivery of the *Scythia* and *Samaria*.

Laconia, *Franconia* and *Carinthia* were all placed on cruising duties. *Carinthia* proved especially popular, with many passengers booking cruises on her year by year. In her brochures of 1926, *Carinthia* was described as 'the newest Cunard liner, which was designed especially for cruising and is without question the finest cruise ship in the world'. *Laconia* completed the first Round the World cruise in 1922 on charter to American Express. *Franconia* was also advertised as offering a Round the World cruise in 1924, *Tuscania* to the West Indies and *Scythia*, *Laconia* and *Samaria* to the Mediterranean. *Mauretania* also cruised to Egypt in 1924.

Frank Tourist Company of New York advertised their '50th Anniversary Cruise de Luxe' to the Mediterranean on the *Scythia*. She sailed from New York on 29 January 1925 with 400 guests, which was less than half her capacity. The cruise celebrated Frank's Golden Jubilee on *Scythia*, which 'is a veritable floating palace, with spacious decks, lounges, veranda cafés, 2 elevators, gymnasium, commodious staterooms with running water and large wardrobes; bedrooms and suites with private baths. The famous Cunard cuisine and service with only one sitting for meals.'

The Cunard and Anchor Steam Ship lines offered two thirty-day Caribbean cruises on *Tuscania* sailing from New York on 22 January and 24 February 1925. The cruises called at Havana, Kingston, Colon, Cartagena, Curaçao, La Guayra, Port of Spain, Barbados, Martinique, St Thomas, San Juan, Nassau and Barbados. *Mauretania* was also advertised to operate a cruise from New York to Egypt and the Mediterranean on 17 February that year. *Carinthia* sailed from New York on 14 October 1926 on a 151-day 'Cruise around the World'.

Franconia was chartered by Thos Cook for several cruises in 1927. She sailed from New York on 12 January and Los Angeles on 29 January, returning to New York on 2 June. The cruise was billed as 'Cooks Cruise Supreme Around the World via the Southern Hemisphere' and featured modern cities hidden in remote worlds, hillside plantations – the aroma of spices, tremendous waterfalls, gold, diamonds mined before your very eyes – and so on around the entire world – Honolulu, South Seas, New Zealand, Tasmania, Australia, East Indies, Ceylon, East Africa, South Africa and South America.

In co-operation with Thos Cook the Cunard Line organised a forty-three-day cruise on *Mauretania*, for $830 and upwards. She sailed from New York on 21 February 1927 and called at Madeira, Gibraltar, Algiers, Villefranche, Naples, Athens, Haifa (Holy Land), Alexandria and Southampton. At the end of her career, from 1930 to 1935, *Mauretania* was employed mainly on cruising duties and was painted white in 1931.

Scythia's fifth annual deluxe cruise was limited to 400 guests and sailed on 26 January 1927 to Madeira, Spain, Gibraltar, Algiers, Tunis, Palermo, Messina, Taormina, Syracuse, Malta, Constantinople, Greece, Venice, Naples, Riviera, Monte Carlo, France and then to England. The brochure advertised it thus:

The cruise of the magnificent 20,000 ton *Scythia* to the Mediterranean, under special charter, has become an annual classic. In every respect it is unsurpassed. Hot and cold running water in each cabin. Prearranged shore excursions at every port, included in the rate. Finest hotels and the best of everything. Unusually long stay at the height of the season, in Egypt and Palestine.

A stopover privilege in Europe was offered at no extra cost, returning via SS *Aquitania*, *Mauretania*, *Berengaria* or any Cunard Line steamer. Cunard Mediterranean Winter Cruises sent the 17,000-ton *Lancastria* from Southampton on a twenty-two-day cruise to the Mediterranean on 5 March 1927. It was her second cruise that that year and prices ranged from £40.

Canadian Pacific's *Empress of Australia*'s world cruise, sailing from New York on 2 December 1927, was advertised as '133 days – the wonder belt of the world'. *Empress of Australia* was claimed to be 'a dream ship, from the power of her mighty engines to the luxury of her bath roomed suites, public lounges and swimming pool.' The cruise included calls at twenty-six ports in nineteen countries, '133 days of summer all the way. The path begins in the Mediterranean. It then goes through the Holy Land and Egypt. It covers India and China, and ends in Japan. A veritable belt, a wonder belt, around the world.'

Red Star Line's *Belgenland* embarked on a 133-day world cruise on 4 December 1924. She carried out a number of Mediterranean cruises in 1933 and later some voyages from London. After being laid up at London, she was sold to the Atlantic Transport Company in 1935 and renamed *Columbia* for the New York–California service, via the Panama Canal. The service proved uneconomic and she was placed on the New York–West Indies route, via Miami and Havana. This also proved unsuccessful and she was laid up and sold for scrap the following year.

Although the Great Depression, which began in 1929, did not affect most of the wealthiest travellers, the steamship companies were forced to look for alternative revenue, such as cruising, to enable to ships to continue to operate. Work on the new *Queen Mary* (534) ceased in 1931, with the British government having to advance £3 million to complete her two years later. There was to be another loan of £5 million if a sister was to be built to run alongside her, and the assistance was conditional upon the merging of the White Star Line with Cunard. The merger was effective from February 1934, creating Cunard-White Star Line. Work resumed on '534' and she was launched as *Queen Mary* on 26 September 1934. People were also able to experience cruising when the shipping companies offered short cruises from American, Canadian and British ports during the layover periods between line voyages.

An advertisement in 1931 offered a Round the World cruise organised by the Cunard Line, P&O and the British India Steam Navigation Company Limited. It was from New York and London to Marseilles, Egypt, Sudan, India, Pakistan, Persian Gulf, Burma, Ceylon, China, Japan, East and South Africa, Mauritius and Australasia. British India Line introduced educational cruises in 1932, with *Neuralia* sailing to the Norwegian fjords. She carried around 1,100 pupils and their teachers on each fourteen-day cruise to Bergen, Stavanger, Kristiansand, Oslo, Copenhagen and the Kiel Canal. Two Baltic cruises were offered the following year, returning to the Norwegian fjords in 1934.

When the revenue from the North Atlantic passenger trade began to drop in 1921, the Anchor Line had been offering cruises from New York to Nassau and Havana. They also organised 'booze' cruises from New York during the prohibition period in the United States, and some of these were advertised as 'Cruises to Nowhere'. *Caledonia*, *Transylvania* and *Tuscania* were operated by the shipping line in the off season, with *Transylvania* providing an eighty-eight-day Round the World cruise in 1931.

The Royal Mail cruising liner *Atlantis* sailed from Southampton to the Islands and West Africa on 20 December 1935. The fares started at 35 guineas for the twenty-day cruise. The Blue Star liner *Arandora Star* left Southampton on the same day for a twenty-day cruise with fares also from 35 guineas. The following day the Lamport & Holt vessel *Voltaire* left Southampton for Portugal, Morocco and the Atlantic Isles. The fare was from 20 guineas for the fifteen-day cruise. The new P&O liner *Strathmore* sailed from London on 21 December for a twenty-day cruise to the Atlantic Isles, West Africa, Morocco and Spain with fares from 35 guineas.

Leaving Southampton on 27 December 1935, the Cunard White Star liner *Franconia* visited New York, Trinidad, Brazil, St Helena, South Africa, Madagascar, Seychelles, India, Ceylon, Bali, Java, Malaya, Siam, Philippines, Hong Kong, China, Japan, Hawaii, Panama and New York, returning to Southampton on 8 June. Fares for the voyage were from

395 guineas, which included all the organised shore excursions. The following day, P&O's *Viceroy of India* sailed on a seventy-three-day cruise from London to visit India, Ceylon, Penang, Singapore and the East Indies, with fares from £135.

The P&O liner *Strathmore* sailed from London on 11 January 1936 to call at Madeira, Jamaica, Trinidad, Barbados, Santa Cruz and Casablanca. *Empress of Britain* left Monaco on 22 January to cruise to Naples, Athens, Haifa, Port Said, Suez, Bombay, Colombo, Penang, Singapore, Bangkok, Batavia, Semarang, Bali, Manila, Hong Kong, Shanghai, Chinwangtao, Beppu, Kobe, Yokohama, Honolulu, Hilo, San Francisco, Los Angeles, Balbao, Cristobal, Havana and New York. She returned to Southampton on 26 May.

Stella Polaris left Harwich on 5 January 1936 on a world cruise, and returned to Southampton on 7 May. The Pacific Steam Navigation Company passenger vessel *Reina del Pacifico* sailed from Liverpool on 15 January, calling at Plymouth the following day. She sailed to France, Spain, Gran Canaria, Brazil, Uruguay, Argentina, Falkland Islands, Magellan Straits, Chile, Juan Fernandez, Peru and the Panama Canal, returning via Jamaica, Cuba, Bahamas and Bermuda and arriving at Plymouth on 29 March and at Liverpool on the following day. Fares were from £140 first class and £105 second class.

The Lamport & Holt white sisters *Voltaire* and *Vandyck* left Southampton and Liverpool on 9 April 1936 on cruises of eighteen days each at fares from 24 guineas each. However, the only joint port of call was Lisbon. The *Voltaire* visited Gibraltar, Casablanca, Santa Cruz de la Palma and Madeira, while *Vandyck*'s other calls were Ceuta, Villefranche and Palma. In the Easter of 1936, *Atlantis* of the Royal Mail Line travelled to Ceuta, Phaleron Bay, Gallipoli, Istanbul, Malta and Lisbon, with the cruise lasting twenty-three days and fares from 40 guineas. *Arandora Star* left Southampton on 9 April for a twenty-five-day cruise to Bizerta

(Tunis), Rhodes, Famagusta, Beirut, Haifa, Jaffa, Port Said, Alexandria, Philipville and Lisbon.

The Orient Line vessel *Orontes* sailed from London on 24 April for a twenty-one-day cruise to Malta, Famagusta, Port Said, Alexandria, Philipville and Lisbon, and five Yeoward Line cruises from Liverpool ranged from seventeen days at 17 guineas to nineteen days at 19 guineas.

The event of the 1936 season was the maiden voyage of the Cunard liner *Queen Mary* from Southampton on 27 May. So great was the demand for accommodation that after the 2,500 berths had been fully booked, the Cunard White Star Line were forced to turn down more than 1,000 applicants. While the *Queen Mary* was making nautical history, the lesser lights of the Cunard White Star Line were keeping the flag flying in other directions. The *Lancastria*, after her April Scholars' cruise, made a twenty-two-day trip to Gallipoli and Salonika, a trip which had a wider appeal to those interested in the Near East Campaign during the First World War. She left Liverpool on 1 May, calling at Malta, Istanbul and Gibraltar, and on arrival at Gallipoli there was a special excursion to Helles and a visit to the battlefields.

Nine other cruises were undertaken by *Lancastria* between May and October 1936, varying in length from twelve to sixteen days with rates from £15 to £20 depending on the length of the cruises, which were to the Mediterranean and northern capitals. An innovation by the Cunard White Star Line was the arrangement made for parties comprising ten or more holidaymakers to be personally conducted on tours. The first tours took place at Easter, with the party leaving in the *Aquitania* on 8 April, and after a seven-day stay in New York they returned on *Georgic*, which left New York on 20 April.

A party left on 11 July sailing on *Britannic*, and after eleven days ashore, during which they visited New York, Niagara, Washington, Philadelphia and Atlantic City, they returned by the *Queen Mary* from New York on 29

July. Another party left Southampton for Canada on the *Alaunia* on 25 July for an eleven-day tour visiting Quebec, Montreal, Ottawa, Toronto, Niagara Falls, Albany and New York, from where the return voyage was made by *Queen Mary*. For passengers wishing to do a round voyage to New York or Canada, arrangements were made for a seventeen-hour stay in connection with all sailings.

One of the major shipping magazines of the time wrote,

The P&O Line are in such an enviable position to tap enormous supplies of sunshine that they are able to hand out complete suns with their cruising booklets. The finely produced illustrations constitute a cruise in imagination – a wise thought to place the street of what appears to be ten million steps, at Malta, in the centre of the book, following a lazy time amid less energetic scenes, and followed by several good impressions of a Lotus-Eater's Paradise. The love tree overlooking the mist dimmed sea at Ninamar simply invites one to a long siesta.

Twenty voyages were made by ships of the P&O Line in 1936, varying in itineraries catering for widely different tastes, and they also varied in length from 2,900 to 6,400 miles. The *Viceroy of India* sailed from London on 19 June for Leith, Trondhjem, Nurmansk, North Cape, Isoniso, Narvik and Bergen. From London to London the fares were from 21 guineas, and from Leith to Leith from 18 guineas; the cruise lasted fourteen days. On her Norwegian Fjords cruise from London on 4 July *Viceroy of India* called at fourteen Norwegian ports after leaving Leith. At four of them she did not stay, merely calling to pick up or land passengers taking overland excursions. *Viceroy of India* also offered a thirteen-day Atlantic Isles and Spain cruise in August and a twenty-one-day Southampton to Constantinople, Grecian Archipelago and North Africa cruise on 29 August 1936.

Canadian Pacific enticed prospective passengers to:

Try a Canadian Pacific Cruise or Tour overseas, the new, fashionable holiday mode that provides the maximum pleasure for people with limited leisure. The Canadian Pacific cruising fleet includes SS *Empress of Australia*, the famous 22,000 ton 'Dreamship of Cruises'. First class only, limited membership. SS *Duchess of Atholl*, SS *Duchess of Richmond*. Splendid modern 20,000 ton cruising liners, SS *Montcalm, Monclare* and *Montrose*. Popular 16,400 ton liners specially equipped for cruising. One class only. Fares from £1 a day.

They also offered to help plan a 'New World Holiday' or to join one of the accompanied tours (eighteen to thirty-two days), which left nearly every week from early April to late September. The itineraries covered Quebec, Montreal, Ottawa, Niagara Falls, French River, New York and Chicago. Special all-in fares covered the complete cost, including the Atlantic crossing both ways by the short sea route 'with a splendid 1,000 miles smooth water cruise through the picturesque St Lawrence seaway'.

Montcalm sailed from Liverpool on 2 May 1936 for a thirteen-day cruise to Gibraltar, Barcelona, Palma and Lisbon. On the day following her return, she left for Tangier, Tarragona, Barcelona, Palma and Cadiz, and again on 30 May to Madeira, Las Palmas, Tenerife and Lisbon. Another Mediterranean cruise followed on 13 June and also on 27 June, five cruises with only a day at home between each and fares from £1 a day. *Montclare* made one cruise from Southampton to Copenhagen, Leningrad, Helsingfors, Stockholm, Loppot and Travemunde.

Britannic took a fifteen-day cruise to Havana from New York on 18 December 1936, *Berengaria* followed on a five-day New Year's Cruise to Nassau. On her return, *Britannic* sailed on two six-day cruises to the West Indies on 8 and 16 January 1937. *Carinthia* was advertised as sailing every Saturday to Nassau from 23 January to 6 March 1937. *Georgic's* programme of cruises from New York included two to Havana and Nassau on 9 and 23 January and two eighteen-day voyages to the West Indies and South America on 6 and 27 February 1937.

Shorter cruises were offered by the Blue Funnel Line on their services between London and Glasgow, via the north and west coasts of Scotland. The trip lasted six days, including two days in Holland, and cost 7 guineas. Passengers could also travel on longer trips by Blue Funnel steamer to the Canary Islands for £17 return, while the more ambitious could make an inclusive tour to Cairo, having twenty-two days at sea and three or four days in Egypt from £40.

The United Baltic Corporation Limited were responsible for fortnightly sailings from London, via the Kiel Canal, to Baltic seaside resorts. A point of interest on these steamers was that dressing for dinner was optional and the fares were £12 for eleven days. Seventeen days in the Land of the Pharaohs were offered by the Bibby Line on an Egyptian tour for £76 from Liverpool and back to Plymouth or London. The Bibby Line also offered specially reduced return fares to holidaymakers wishing to visit the East. From Liverpool to Egypt, return fares were £47, Sudan £63, Cochin or Ceylon £85, Burma £100 and the Straits Settlements £111. Bibby Line vessels were all first class only.

The West Coast of Africa once had a bad name with travellers but the efforts of the Elder Dempster Lines achieved much in the development of the region. By the mid- and late 1930s, Elder Dempster Lines were operating holiday tours to West Africa. In addition, tours to Madeira and the Canary Islands could be made on their regular services at specially reduced fares of £20 first saloon and £15 second saloon. The Henderson Line vessels made regular calls at Gibraltar and holidaymakers could travel on their ships for £14 return. Palma, on the isle of Majorca, could be visited for £18 return and the trip to Marseilles was £19 return.

Henderson's also offered cruise holiday prices for the voyage to Egypt, Sudan and Burma.

Cunard White Star advertised a forty-day cruise by *Aquitania* from New York on 17 February 1936 as 'the largest liners to sail below the equator'. The cruise included calls at Rio de Janeiro, Buenos Aires, Montevideo, Nassau, Panama, La Guira, Barbados and Trinidad. It was advertised as costing $495 upwards. *Empress of Britain's* world cruise of 1937 from New York lasted 128 days.

The *Wilhelm Gustloff* was the first purpose-built cruise liner for the German Labour Front. She was designed and built to provide recreational and cultural activities for German officials and workers, including concerts, cruises and holidays. She was followed by the *Robert Ley* and operated Hitler's 'Strength through Joy' scheme for the German Workers Front. *Wilhelm Gustloff* was sunk on 30 January 1945 by the Soviet submarine S-13 with a spread of three torpedoes. She sank within fifty minutes, with a loss of 9,343 lives. It was the largest loss of life in a single sinking in maritime history.

Cruising was very popular right up to the beginning of the Second World War. Cunard White Star advertised *Britannic* as sailing from New York to Nassau, Bahamas, on 8 March 1939, *Georgic* on 18 March, 29 March and 7 April and *Lancastria* every Saturday from 6 May to 16 December on 'no passport' eight-day cruises from $97.50 upwards and six-day cruises from $55.00 upwards.

Lancastria later offered 22-guinea cruises from Liverpool to Gibraltar, Tangiers, Villefranche and Lisbon. *Franconia* visited forty ports on her five-month Round the World cruise. This took her from Southampton to New York, the Caribbean, South America, South Africa, India, Singapore, Hong Kong, Darwin and across the Pacific to San Francisco, the Panama Canal, New York and Liverpool.

Cape of Good Hope was the first vessel in the British India fleet. She was built in 1856 for the General Screw Company's service from London to South Africa and was bought by the Calcutta & Burmah Steam Navigation Company for the Calcutta–Moulmein route. Following her arrival, she was used as a troopship during the Indian mutiny in 1856–57 and found employment on the Trincomalee–Bombay and Calcutta service. On 23 March 1859 she collided with the P&O vessel *Nemasis* in the River Hooghly with 145 people on board. There was no loss of life and she later became owned by the British India Line.

Gallia was a sister of *Bothnia* and *Scythia* and sailed on her maiden voyage on 5 April 1879 from Liverpool to New York. She holds the distinction of being the last ship built for the British & North American Royal Mail Steam Packet Company before it became the Cunard Line. She was operating to Boston in 1886 and on the intermediate service to New York during 1889. Her propeller shaft gave her problems in 1895 and she was towed to Liverpool by the *River Afton*. The following year she was chartered to carry troops to Cuba and renamed *Don Alvado de Bazan*. She returned to Cunard service in 1897 when she was sold to D. & C. MacIver to operate on the Beaver Line services to Halifax and St Johns, New Brunswick. The fleet was transferred to the Elder Dempster Line in 1898 and sold to the Allan Line in 1900. However, she grounded near Sorel Point, Quebec, on 18 May that year and was salvaged and returned to Liverpool, where she was declared beyond economic repair and scrapped at Cherbourg.

Tanjore was built by the Thames Iron Works at London in 1865 for the P&O Line and sailed on her maiden voyage on 15 August that year. Her owners were so pleased with her engines and how economical they were that they re-engined *Ceylon, Columbian, China* and *Peru*. She was fitted with new boilers and a poop in 1870 and was transferred to the Bombay service, via the Suez Canal, three years later. She was re-engined at Glasgow in 1876 and four years later she became a refugee ship in Alexandria during the Arabi Pasha dispute. In 1888 she was laid up at Bombay and sold the following year to be used to take pilgrims to Mecca.

Above: Wisconsin.

Left: Cuzco was one of five similar sisters built for the Pacific Steam Navigation Company. She cost £90,000 and sailed on her maiden voyage on 13 January 1872. Five years later she was chartered to operate on the Orient Pacific Line service from London to Sydney, via the Suez Canal. In 1878 she was sold to the Orient Steam Navigation Company and retained the same name. She was fitted with triple-expansion engines by her builder in 1888 and survived until 1905 when she was broken up at Genoa.

STEAM TO RIO DE JANEIRO AND VALPARAISO

The Pacific Steam Navigation Company's Royal Mail new iron Steam Ship

NEW GRENADA

of 600 tons burthen and 200 horse-power

Captain John Williams, Commander:
(who is well acquainted with the trade)

will leave Liverpool for:

RIO DE JANEIRO AND VALPARAISO

on an early day of this month

The NEW GRENADA has very spacious accommodation for passengers, and as only a limited number will be taken, an early application for berths will be necessary. No goods will be carried. For particulars as to passage, etc. apply at the Company's offices.

William Taggart, Secretary·

Fenwick Chambers, Liverpool
2nd September, 1846

N.B. the day of sailing will be named in a future advertisement.

FOR MADEIRA, RIO DE JANEIRO, AND VALPARAISO.

To Sail on WEDNESDAY, the 28th JULY next,

The Pacific Steam Navigation Company's Royal Mail Iron Steam-ship

PRINCE OF WALES,

Of 700 tons, and 200 horse-power;
W. H. Ellis, Commander.

This vessel has excellent accommodation for Passengers. For terms of passage or freight of treasure (no other description of cargo will be taken), apply at the Company's office, No. 27, James-street, Liverpool; or in London to Messrs. Griffiths, Tate, and Fisher, White Hart-court.

26th June, 1858.   WILLIAM TAGGART, Secretary.

N.B.—Passengers for the undermentioned Ports will have an opportunity of leaving Valparaiso by the contract mail packets of the Company on the 1st or 16th of each month, namely, Coquimbo, Huasco, Caldera (Copiapo), Cobija, Iquique, Arica, Islay, Pisco, Callao, Huacho, Casma, Huanchaco, Lambayeque, Payta, Guayaquil, and Panama.

Above: 1858 advert for the Pacific Steam Navigation Company vessel *Prince of Wales.*

Left: Pacific Steam Navigation Company advert, 1846.

Above: Saloon on *Liguria*, 1874. *Liguria* was a sister of *Iberia* and was introduced in 1874 on the South American route. She was transferred to the Orient Line's Australian service in 1880 and operated via the Suez Canal to Melbourne and Sydney for ten years before returning to the Valparaiso service. She was also re-engined in 1893 and was broken up at Genoa in 1903.

Left: Iberia was built by John Elder & Company at Glasgow in 1873. She was launched as the world's largest ship excepting *Great Eastern,* but was delayed entering service until the following year because of labour disputes at the shipyard. She was also placed on the joint Orient-Pacific Steam Navigation Company service in 1880 and was requisitioned by the Admiralty in 1882 during the Egyptian Arabi Pasha dispute. She returned to the Australian service the following year and was transferred to the Liverpool–Valparaiso route in 1890. Three years later she was fitted with triple-expansion engines at Liverpool, and during a positioning voyage to Australia in 1895 she took thirty-two days to complete the voyage from the United Kingdom. She was broken up at Genoa in 1903.

Above left: Liguria.

Above right: Dorunda and her sister *Merkara* were built by William Denny & Brothers at Dumbarton in 1875 for the British India Line. In 1881 she was operating on the London–Brisbane service, and in 1884 she transported the first shipment of frozen meat from Brisbane to England. She was wrecked at Peniche, off Portugal, on 7 December 1894.

Right: The Cunard liner *Damascus* (1856, 1,214 grt).

Left: Orotava was built by the Barrow Shipbuilding Company in 1889 for the Pacific Steam Navigation Company's Liverpool–Valparaiso service but was transferred to the Orient Line route to Australia after only two round voyages. She capsized while coaling at Tilbury in 1896 and resumed service the following year. From 1899 to 1903, during the Boer War, she became transport No. 91, returning to the Australian route in 1903. Three years later she was owned by the Royal Mail Line and remained on the Australia station until 1909. For the majority of the First World War she was a member of the 10th Cruiser Squadron and was broken up in 1919 at the end of hostilities.

Right: Campania sailed on her maiden voyage to New York for the Cunard Line on 22 April 1893. She took the Blue Riband on her second voyage and made her fastest crossing in five days, nine hours and twenty-one minutes in August 1894. She was at the Diamond Jubilee Spithead review on 26 July 1897. *Campania* suffered a number of unfortunate incidents in her career. She sank a small sailing vessel in 1900 and eleven people were lost, and was hit by a large wave in heavy seas in 1904 when five people were washed overboard and thirty others were injured. She was taken out of service in 1914 and chartered to the Anchor Line for several sailings. However, she returned to service at the outbreak of the First World War for several voyages from Liverpool to New York. Following these, she was sold to be broken up. Requisitioned by the Admiralty later in 1914, she was sent to be converted to an Armed Merchant Cruiser by Cammell Laird, and during the work a flight platform was installed forward. A hangar was also fitted on the bridge top. The following year she was sent back to Cammell Laird's and her fore funnel was split and the flight deck extended, with a hangar beneath. Following a successful war career she broke from her moorings in the Firth of Forth on 5 November 1918, collided with the battleship *Revenge* and sank. All on board were rescued by other vessels.

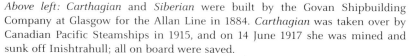

Above left: Carthagian and *Siberian* were built by the Govan Shipbuilding Company at Glasgow for the Allan Line in 1884. *Carthagian* was taken over by Canadian Pacific Steamships in 1915, and on 14 June 1917 she was mined and sunk off Inishtrahull; all on board were saved.

Above right: Caledonia was owned by P&O Line and entered service in 1894 with yellow funnels and a white hull. She retained this livery for two years, and in 1903 was the first P&O ship to use Tilbury Dock. In December 1916, she was mined off Marseille but suffered little damage. She was sold in Bombay in 1925 and broken up.

Right: P&O's *Ophir* leaving Portsmouth on 16 March 1901 with the Duke and Duchess of York on board. She was painted white for the royal tour; her first call was Australia, where the Duke opened the first Commonwealth parliament. The 45,000-mile voyage took seven months.

Left: Trial cruise on *Tantallon Castle*, 1894. She was built in 1894 for the Union Castle Line and in June the following year she cruised with guests at the opening of the Kiel Canal.

Below: Macedonia sailed on her maiden voyage from London to Bombay for the P&O Line on 12 February 1904, and was later placed on the Australian service. She also operated on a route from China to Britain in 1907, and was converted to an Armed Merchant Cruiser in 1914. In this role she operated closely with HMS *Bristol* at the Battle of the Falkland Islands, and in 1916 she was chartered by the Admiralty. She was returned to P&O in 1921 and, following an extensive conversion, she was placed on their Far Eastern route. She was broken up in Japan in 1931.

P AND O

s.s. "MACEDONIA."
10,512 Tons.   15,000 h.p.

Devanha was built for the P&O Line in 1906 and operated on their Indian and Far Eastern service. In 1915 she was operating at Anzac Beach, Gallipoli, landing troops and acting as a hospital ship. She was the last vessel to leave the beaches, and on 5 April 1916 she took survivors to Malta from Chantala, which had been torpedoed. At the end of the war she was placed on the Far East service with an occasional voyage to Australia, and was scrapped in 1928.

Ascania was one of six 'A' class vessels built for the Cunard Line services to Canada. She was completed in 1925 and was placed on the company's service from London. In 1939 she was requisitioned by the Admiralty as an Armed Merchant Cruiser and became a Landing Ship in 1942. On 9 July 1943 she participated in the invasion of Sicily and then the Anzio landings. She later operated as a troopship and was returned to Cunard's Liverpool–Halifax service in 1947. In 1950 she was operating from Liverpool to Quebec and Montreal and carried troops to Cyprus during the Suez Crisis in 1956. She was broken up at Newport in 1957.

Left: Ranchi was built in 1925 for P&O's Bombay service. She became an Armed Merchant Cruiser during the Second World War and was converted to a troopship in 1943. *Ranchi* was returned to service in 1948 without her second funnel and employed on Australian emigrant service with accommodation for 950 people. She left the United Kingdom on her final sailing to Australia on 6 October 1952 and was broken up the following year at Newport.

Below: Vandyck was built by Workman Clark at Belfast for the Lamport & Holt Line. She was launched on 24 February 1921 but her delivery was delayed because of vibration problems discovered on her trials. In 1922 she completed a voyage for the Royal Mail Line on the Hamburg–New York route. In 1932 she and her sister ship *Voltaire* were converted for cruising service and both were painted with a white hull. They were employed on this service during the 1930s, and at the outbreak of war in 1939 she was converted to an Armed Boarding Cruiser, as HMS *Vandyck*. She later became an Accommodation ship and Depot ship, and in 1940 took part in the Norwegian campaign. She was damaged by enemy aircraft on 9 June 1940 and was abandoned the following day when the fire on board took hold. She sank on 11 June following further attacks by German fighter aircraft.

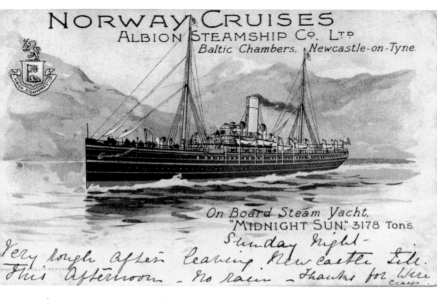

Above: Norway cruises have always been popular. A postcard from the Albion Line used in 1898.

Right: Queen Mary is probably the most famous Cunard liner. She was built by John Brown & Company on the Clyde and was laid down as yard number 534 on 27 December 1930. However, later the following year work ceased because of the financial depression, and it was not until 1934 that the construction was restarted and she was launched by Queen Mary on 26 September that year. She left Southampton on her maiden voyage to New York on 27 May 1936 and took the westbound Blue Riband with a voyage time of four days, twenty-seven minutes, and then the eastbound record in three days, twenty-three hours and fifty-seven minutes. She was laid up in New York for six months in 1939 and left for Sydney on 20 March 1940 to be converted to a troopship. Her final trooping duties were in 1946 and it was estimated that she carried over 810,000 people during the course of the Second World War. *Queen Mary* resumed service on the North Atlantic on 31 July 1947 and left New York for the final time on 22 September 1967. She sailed from Southampton on 31 October with 1,000 passengers after being purchased by the City of Long Beach in California, arriving there on 9 December, and was converted to a museum, hotel and convention centre.

Aurania at Liverpool landing stage. She was the fourth of the 'A' class vessels built for the Canadian service and was delivered in 1925. During the Second World War she was converted to an Armed Merchant Cruiser and also carried out some trooping duties. In July 1941 she had a slight collision with an iceberg between Iceland and Halifax and was later torpedoed but managed to limp back to Scotland. Following a lay-up she was converted to a Heavy Repair Ship and renamed *Artifex*. Re-boilered in 1948 she continued in service until 1961 when she was sold to be broken up at La Spezia.

Aquitania was another product of John Brown's shipyard at Glasgow. She was delivered in 1914 to operate a weekly service across the Atlantic with *Mauretania* and *Lusitania*. She was requisitioned by the Admiralty in 1914 and converted into an Armed Merchant Cruiser, but following trials in the Irish Sea she was laid up at Liverpool. In May 1915 she was used as a troopship and carried over 30,000 men to the Dardanelles, later operating as a hospital ship. She was laid up at Liverpool for most of 1917 and the following year she carried out trooping duties across the North Atlantic. She returned to service in February 1919 on the Liverpool–New York service and was converted to burn diesel oil later that year. In 1924 she carried out a number of cruises from New York and ran in conjunction with *Queen Mary* when she entered service in 1936. In 1939 she became a troopship, and at the end of the Second World War she was used to carry United States troops back to America. She was also used by the Canadian Government to carry out voyages from Southampton to Halifax in 1948. After being laid up for a short time she was sold and broken up at Faslane in 1950.

Above: Wilhelm Gustloff, a dedicated cruise ship from Germany visited London in 1938.

Right from top to the bottom:
William Fawcett was built in 1829 and was designed to operate as a Mersey ferry between Liverpool and Runcorn. She was sold to the Dublin & London Steam Packet Company in 1831 and chartered to the Peninsular Steam Line in 1835 for the London–Madeira service.

Hindostan was built for the P&O Line in 1842 for their Southampton–Gibraltar–Cape Verde–Ascension–St Helena–Cape Town–Mauritius–Galle–Calcutta route. She was visited by Queen Victoria and Prince Albert on 16 July 1849 when off Osborne, Isle of Wight, and was chartered by the Madras government in 1860 for trooping duties in China. She became a store ship at Calcutta in 1862 and sank during the Great Cyclone at Calcutta on 5 October 1864.

Lady Mary Wood was built by Thomas Wilson at Liverpool and was delivered for P&O's Mediterranean services in 1842. Three years later she was transferred to the Ceylon–Singapore–Hong Kong route. In 1848 she became the first steam troopship when she took men to Ceylon following a revolt. In 1850 she was placed on a new Hong Kong–Shanghai service. However, the service was unsuccessful because of opposition from local shipping interests at Shanghai and she was sold in 1859 to Indonesia.

Bentinck was a sister of *Hindostan* and operated on the route to Calcutta, via the Suez Canal. In 1860 she was sold to the Calcutta government and converted to an armed merchant vessel.

Above: Teutonic was a product of Harland & Wolff at Belfast and was delivered in 1889 to the White Star Line for the Liverpool–Queenstown–New York route. She participated in Queen Victoria's Diamond Review at Spithead on 26 June 1897 and was used as a Boer War transport during 1900. She was based at Southampton in 1907 and was rebuilt in 1911. Taken over by the Admiralty in 1914 as an Armed Merchant Cruiser, she was attached to the 10th Cruiser Squadron. In 1917 she was used as an escort and the following year she carried out trooping duties to Alexandria. She was laid up in 1921 and broken up at Emden.

Right: Majestic was delivered to the White Star Line in 1890 to replace *Republic*. She operated as a Boer War transport from Liverpool to Cape Town in 1899 and Southampton to Cape Town the following year. During 1902–03 she received a major overhaul at her builders at Belfast when her funnels were heightened. She was also transferred to Southampton in 1907 and became reserve vessel four years later, when she was laid up in Bidston Dock, Birkenhead. Following the *Titanic* disaster *Majestic* was brought back into service. She made her final sailing to New York on 14 January 1914 and was broken up at Morecambe the following year.

Top left: Liner departs from Prince's Landing Stage, Liverpool.

Bottom left and right: Passenger liners at the landing stage, Liverpool.

Germanic was built by Harland & Wolff at Belfast in 1875 for White Star Line's service to New York. In January 1883 she was diverted to Waterford when her propeller shaft snapped, and in 1895 triple-expansion engines and new boilers were fitted during a major overhaul and refit. She was the first ship to embark passengers at Liverpool's new landing stage on 15 May 1895. On 13 February 1899 she capsized at New York while she was coaling. She was salvaged and sent to Belfast for repairs. In 1904 she was transferred to the American Line and later to the Dominion Line. She became *Ottawa* the following year, operating from Liverpool to Halifax, Quebec and Montreal. She was sold to the government of Turkey in 1910 and the following year she was carrying troops to the Yemen. On 3 May 1915 she was torpedoed while at anchor in the Sea of Marmora with a major loss of life among the troops who were on board. She repatriated German troops from Turkey in 1918 and was operating for the Ottoman-America Line during 1920–21. She was renamed *Gulcemal* in 1928 and went aground in 1931, becoming a store ship at Istanbul and later a floating hotel. She was broken up in 1950.

Cedric was also built by Harland & Wolff at Belfast and was delivered to White Star Line in 1903. In 1906 she was employed cruising from New York to the Mediterranean and repeated these in the winter of 1911. She was in New York in 1913 when *Titanic* sank and her departure was delayed to enable survivors to return to England if they wished. In 1914 she was converted to an Armed Merchant cruiser and later in the First World War she was engaged on trooping duties. On 29 January 1918 she was in collision and sank the Canadian Pacific steamer *Montreal* in convoy near the Mersey Bar. She was also in collision with the Cunard liner *Scythia* in 1923. Sold for breaking up at Inverkeithing in 1932, and replaced by the motorship *Britannic*.

Above left: Megantic was a sister of *Laurentic* and was laid down as *Albany* for the Dominion Line. She sailed on her maiden voyage from Liverpool to Montreal on 17 June 1909. In 1915 she became a troopship and returned to commercial service in 1918 on the Liverpool–New York route. In the winter of 1919 she operated a number of cruises from New York to the West Indies, and the following year she sailed on one voyage to Sydney and Wellington on the joint White Star–Shaw Savill service. She was chartered in 1927 to take troops to Shanghai and the following year was placed on the London–Le Havre–Halifax–New York service and to Quebec and Montreal in the summer. During 1930–31 she operated a number of economy cruises with *Adriatic*, *Calgaric* and *Laurentic*. She returned to the Liverpool–Quebec–Montreal service in 1931 and was broken up at Osaka two years later.

Above: Orcoma was built at Glasgow in 1908 for the Pacific Steam Navigation Company. She was the largest and fastest ship on the South American Pacific service and operated a Thomas Cook tour of South America in 1909. She was requisitioned as an Armed Merchant cruiser during the First World War, returning to service in November 1919. Converted to oil fuel in 1923 and broken up at Blyth in 1933. She was replaced by *Reina del Pacifico*.

Left: 1909 P&O Pleasure Cruises advertisement.

Right: Aquitania and *Olympic* at Southampton, taken from *Leviathan.*Both *Aquitania* and *Olympic* undertook cruises in the 1930s

Left: First-class dining saloon on Pacific Steam Navigation's *Orduna* (1914, 15,507 grt).

Opposite, left: A Royal Mail Steam Packet Co. poster for tours to the West Indies.

Opposite, right: Entertainment was ordinarily by the passengers for the passengers with little organised events beyond tours and games such as horse-racing using wooden models. Whist was extremely popular aboard cruise ships, as Bridge is still today.

R.M.S.P.

Cruises
in the
WEST
INDIES
1910.

R.M.S.P.

GENTS

PROGRESSIVE
WHIST

Above: Aquitania at Liverpool landing Stage.

Below and right: Aquitania.

Berengaria was laid down as *Europa* and was launched as *Imperator* by the Kaiser in 1912. She was built for the Hamburg America Line and was the largest ship in the world. When she entered service it was discovered that she was top-heavy and she was sent back to her builder, where 10 feet were taken off her funnels and heavy panelling was replaced with lighter material. At the beginning of the First World War she was laid up in the River Elbe. At the end of hostilities she was used to take American troops home to the United States and was later managed by the Cunard Line as *Imperator*. When she was purchased by them she was renamed *Berengaria* in 1921, converted to oil burning and operated with *Mauretania* and *Aquitania*. On 3 March 1938 she was damaged by fire at New York and returned to Southampton without passengers. It was decided that it would be uneconomic to repair her and she was sold to be broken up at Jarrow. However, the demolition was not completed until after the war ended in 1946.

Left: Armadale Castle, Walmer Castle and *Kenilworth Castle* were three sister ships built by Harland & Wolff at Belfast for the Union Castle Line between 1902 and 1904. *Armadale Castle* sailed from Southampton on her maiden voyage on 5 December 1903, and during the First World War she became an auxiliary cruiser in the 10th Cruiser Squadron. She returned to commercial service in 1918 and was broken up in 1935.

Below left and right: She was laid down as *Amroth Castle* and launched as *Arundel Castle* on 11 September 1919 by Harland & Wolff at Belfast, for the Union Castle Line. She was the company's largest ship and operated on the Southampton–Cape Town service. In 1937 she received a major overhaul and modernisation by her builders when her four funnels were replaced by two. In 1939 she became a troopship and was sunk by a torpedo from an enemy aircraft on 23 March 1943 in the Mediterranean.

Cabin and dining room on the Pacific Steam Navigation vessel *Loreto* (1919, 6,682 grt).

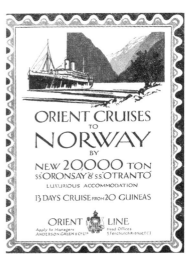

Clockwise, from above: The verandah lounge on *Mauretania.*

Advert for 'The Luxury Cruise – Next Winter' from New York, 10 February 1923 on *Mauretania.*

Aberdeen Steam Navigation Company advert, 1924.

Orient Cruises to Norway.

The *Aberdonian* of the Aberdeen Steam Navigation Co. was used as a hospital ship during the First World War.

Left: A Baltic and Northern Capitals cruise on *Arcadian* from 11 August to 1 September 1928, which called at Oslo, Copenhagen, Wisby, Stockholm, Helingfors, Tallin, Danzig and Hamburg.

Above: *Llanstephan Castle* was built by the Fairfield Ship Building & Engineering Company at Glasgow in 1914. The chairman of the Union Castle Line, Sir Owen Philipps, was lord of the manor of Llanstephan in Wales. She operated on the 'Round Africa' service and was converted to oil burning in 1939. On 8 August 1940 she sailed from Liverpool to Archangel as the commodore ship of the first Allied convoy to Russia and returned with 200 Polish airmen. In 1944 she was operating as a troopship with the Royal Indian Navy and returned to commercial service in 1947. She was sold and broken up in 1952.

Below: A Union Castle vessel in London Docks.

Left: 1931 tours to South Africa advertisement.

The Red Star liner *Belgenland* offered cruises from New York to the Mediterranean in 1924.

COOK'S
1924
MEDITERRANEAN
DE LUXE CRUISE

Sailing Jan. 19—Returning Mar. 26

Including all the scenes of greatest historic, literary and religious interest about the famous Inland Sea.

67 Diverting Days Afloat and Ashore
14,000 Miles

A superb itinerary—by the southern route across the Atlantic to MADEIRA; a long stay in EGYPT—the Valley of the Kings—PALESTINE, etc.

A Plethora of New Features

A la carte Dining Room Service at all hours; private dining rooms for parties; Turkish Baths; Swimming Pool; Gymnasia.

THE SPLENDID, NEW, OIL BURNING,
MAMMOTH STEAMER

"BELGENLAND"

with her broad, glass-enclosed shelter decks, magnificent public-rooms, spacious and airy staterooms has been specially chartered for this cruise and will afford perfection of service and cuisine—the utmost in comfort and luxury.

Stop-over Privileges

in Europe, with return by Majesty, Olympic, Homeric, etc.

Cruise Limited to
500 Guests

preventing any possibility of crowding aboard or ashore.

THOS. COOK & SON

245 Broadway   561 Fifth Ave.
NEW YORK·

| Boston | Philadelphia | Chicago | San Francisco |
| Los Angeles | Montreal | Toronto | Vancouver |

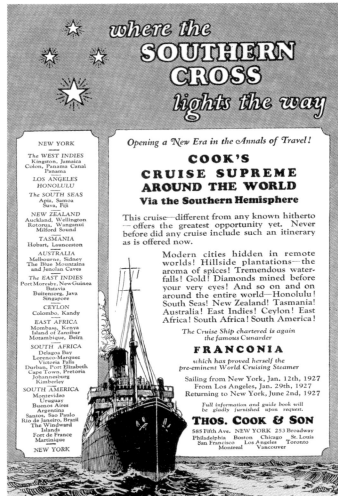

Left: 1926 Orient Line pleasure cruises to Norway, 1926.

Right: Advert for world cruise on *Franconia*, dated June 1926.

Franconia as depicted by one of the best maritime artists of the 1920s and 1930s, Kenneth D. Shoesmith.

The Cunard liners *Caronia* and *Carmania* were built by John Brown at Glasgow in 1905. *Caronia* was employed cruising from New York from 1906 and proved very successful in this role. She was converted to an Armed Merchant Cruiser in 1914 and later in the war she completed trooping duties. She returned to Cunard Line services in 1919 and was converted to oil burning the following year. Following a major overhaul at Barrow in 1924 she emerged with new funnels, and her lifeboats were double banked. She operated from London in the summer and cruised from New York to Havana in the winter months. She was scrapped in 1931.

Carinthia was one of Cunard's most successful cruising vessels of the 1920s and 1930s. On delivery she was placed on the company's Liverpool–New York service and operated cruises out of New York in the winter. In 1930 she was chartered by Furness-Bermuda Line for three months and in 1934 was transferred to the London–New York route. Her hull was painted white in 1935 for cruising out of New York. Converted to an Armed Merchant Cruiser in 1939 and was torpedoed on 6 June 1940 off Ireland by the German U-boat U-46. *Carinthia* remained afloat for thirty-five hours and sank the following day.

Above : Mauretania, Berengaria and *Aquitania.*

Right: Orient Line's *Orsova* was built by John Brown at Glasgow for the London–Suez–Melbourne–Sydney–Brisbane service and was delivered in 1909. She became a troopship in 1915, and on 14 March 1917 she was torpedoed and beached in Cawsand Bay and was later towed to Devonport to be repaired. She returned to Orient Line service in 1919 and was converted to a one-class vessel in 1933. *Orsova* was broken up in 1936.

ORIENT LINE CRUISES

Mediterranean
Adriatic
Egypt
Palestine
Canary Islands
Madeira

Above: Orient Line advert, *c.* 1930.

Right: Orontes was built in 1902 and was owned by the Orient Line who operated her on their route to Australia. She became a troopship in 1916, returning to commercial service at the end of hostilities in 1919. She was laid up in 1921 and sold to become an exhibition ship the following year. However, she was returned to the Orient Line and was broken up in 1926.

PACIFIC LINE

ENGLAND	BERMUDA
FRANCE	JAMAICA
SPAIN	HAVANA

PANAMA CANAL

(For Central American Ports.)

SOUTH AMERICA.

TOURS	THE
ROUND	NEW
SOUTH	TOURING
AMERICA.	GROUND.

THE PACIFIC STEAM NAVIGATION CO., LIVERPOOL.

Left: 1926 Pacific Line advert.

Right: Orduna 'Scouters and Guiders' cruise, 1938.

SCOUTERS' AND GUIDERS' CRUISE

..TO..

ICELAND, NORWAY, DENMARK and BELGIUM

Commencing from LIVERPOOL
MONDAY, 8th AUGUST, 1938

in the Famous Liner

"ORDUÑA"

R.M.S. "ORDUÑA" (15,507 tons gross register).

Schedule of Accommodation and Fares

THE PACIFIC STEAM NAVIGATION COMPANY

Above left: The wide open deck on Pacific Steam Navigation's *Orduna* (1914, 15,507 grt).

Above right: Pacific Steam Navigation Company advert.

Left: Sunny round voyages by popular *Orbita* and *Orduna* advert.

Right: Smoke room on *Orcoma* (1908, 11,546 grt) and table of nautical miles from Liverpool by Pacific Steam Navigation vessels.

Smoke Room, R.M.S. "ORCOMA."

DISTANCES—OUTWARDS VIA STRAITS OF MAGELLAN AND HOMEWARDS VIA PANAMA CANAL.

	Nautical Miles	
	Port to Port	From Liverpool
Liverpool		605
La Rochelle-Pallice	605	965
Coruña	360	1,085
Vigo	120	1,160
Leixoes	75	1,335
Lisbon	175	5,595
Rio de Janeiro	4,260	5,803
Santos	208	6,717
Monte Video	914	7,744
Falkland Islands	1,027	8,303
Punta Arenas	559	9,503
Coronel	1,200	9,546
Talcahuano	43	9,784
Valparaiso	238	10,364
Antofagasta	580	10,424
Mejillones	60	10,604
Iquique	180	10,713
Arica	109	10,845
Mollendo	132	11,303
Callao	458	12,643
Balboa	1,340	12,690
Cristobal	47	13,694
Havana	1,004	17,559
Vigo	3,865	17,679
Coruña	120	17,907
Santander	228	18,103
La Rochelle-Pallice	196	18,453
Plymouth	350	18,807
Liverpool	354	
Miles		18,807

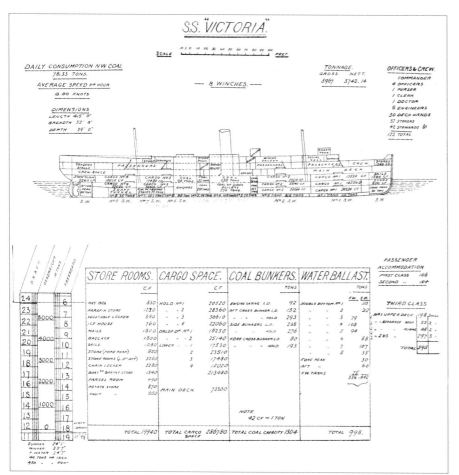

The Pacific Steam Navigation Company's *Victoria* in the River Mersey. She was built in 1903 and was broken up in Holland in 1923.

January 1927 *Mauretania* advertisement. *Mauretania* was another successful Cunard liner that also carried out cruising in the winter months. She was delivered in 1907 and was a sister to *Lusitania*. In 1915 she became a troopship and was later converted to a hospital ship with a white hull and yellow funnel. In 1916 she was painted in camouflage dazzle grey and carried American troops to England from Halifax. She resumed the Liverpool–New York service in 1919 and operated from Southampton the following year. She was damaged by fire at Southampton, converted to oil fuel in 1921 and returned to service the following year. She made a record crossing from Ambrose Light to Cherbourg in 1924 and her hull was painted white for cruising in 1930. In 1934 she completed five cruises out of New York and left there on her final voyage the day that *Queen Mary* was launched. She was broken up at Rosyth in 1935.

Above left and middle: The twin-screw British India Steam Navigation Company passenger liner *Tairea* was built on the Clyde by Barclay Curle & Company Limited for the India & Far East service. Later she was transferred to the Bombay–Africa service before serving as a hospital ship during the Second World War. She was one of the last four ocean-going vessels in the world to carry three funnels, and was broken up at Blyth in 1952.

Right: 1935 'Insure your Baggage' advert.

*A
new holiday
now possible!*

Cruises & Tours

A CHOICE OF ELEVEN FASCINATING CRUISES

"LANCASTRIA" (17,000 tons) from LIVERPOOL

APL. 9 Easter holiday cruise—scholars and adults.
Riviera, Spain, Portugal. **15 days from £18**
Boys £12, Girls £14 including shore excursions.

MAY 1 Early summer cruises to Mediterranean
Gallipoli, Salonika, Near East. **22 days from 24 gns.**

MAY 30 Whitsun cruise to Mediterranean
Portugal and the Riviera. **14 days from £17**

Date	Itinerary	Days	Rates from
June 20	North Africa, Spain, Portugal	13	£16
July 4	North Africa, Canary Isles and Maderia	13	£16
July 18	Norwegian Fjords and Denmark ...	13	£16
Aug. 1	Spain, Riviera, Mediterranean	16	£20
Aug. 22	North Africa, Canary Isles and Maderia	13	£16
Sept. 5	France, Portugal, Maderia, Spain ...	12	£15
Sept. 19	North Africa, Canary Isles and Maderia	13	£16
Oct. 3	North Africa, Spain and Riviera ...	16	£20

TO AMERICA THIS YEAR !

Attractive new programme of tours in U.S.A. and
Canada from 4 to 25 days connecting with regular
sailings including those of Britain's masterpiece
" **QUEEN MARY** "

*Write for cruises and tours programmes to Cunard White
Star Ltd., Liverpool, Manchester, or local offices and agents*

Cunard
White Star

That British Spring!

For three of the worst weeks of the year you
can leave behind the gales of March and its
chilly weather and cruise through the smiling
Mediterranean in genial warmth and leisure.

The 17,000-ton Cunarder 'Lancastria' makes
her second cruise in March.

MARCH 5 from Southampton
22 DAYS. From **£40**

Full particulars of bookings—Cunard Line, Head Office,
Pier Head, Liverpool, or any local Office or Agent.

CUNARD
MEDITERRANEAN
WINTER CRUISES

The Cunard liner *Lancastria* was delivered in 1922
for the company's Canadian services. The following
year she was operating on the Hamburg–New
York route, returning to Liverpool in 1924. In 1936
her hull was painted white for cruising and was
operating the New York–Bermuda service in 1939.
She became a troopship in 1940 and was part of
the evacuation of Narvik during the Norwegian
campaign. On 16 June 1940 she was at St Nazaire
to evacuate troops, refugees and equipment. She
was damaged during intensive bombing and sank
within twenty minutes.

Above left: Bibby Line's *Worcestershire* was delivered in 1931 for the company's passenger and freight service from Liverpool to Rangoon. She was converted to an Armed Merchant Cruiser in 1939 and served on North Atlantic convoy escort duties. She was torpedoed in 1941 but managed to limp back to Liverpool where she was repaired. In 1943 she became a troopship and participated in the Normandy landings in 1944. The following year she was at Malaya and completed various trooping duties in 1946–47 before being returned to her owners. She was broken up in Japan in 1961.

Above right: *Staffordshire* was launched on 29 October 1928 at Glasgow for the Bibby Line's services to Burma. In 1940 she was requisitioned by the Admiralty as a troopship and on 28 March the following year she was bombed by German aircraft near the Outer Hebrides; fourteen passengers and fourteen of her crew lost their lives. The ship was abandoned and the survivors were crowded into the few undamaged lifeboats, but were finally rescued after ten hours at sea. She was beached and later towed to the Tyne to be repaired. She emerged as a troopship and in 1944 took part in the beach landings in the south of France. Later that year she participated in the invasion of Malaya, and returned in 1948 with the 3rd Battalion Grenadier Guards to Singapore. She was rebuilt by the Bibby Line later in 1948 and sold for breaking up in Japan in 1959.

Bibby Line's *Oxfordshire* was delivered in 1912 and was the first British ship to be taken over by the Admiralty in 1914 at the beginning of the First World War. She was converted to a hospital ship at Tilbury. In 1915 she was at the Dardanelles and the following year she was in the Persian Gulf. During 1918 she was used as a hospital ship in the English Channel, and when her war service came to an end it was estimated that she carried the highest number of wounded of any hospital ship in the war. She was converted to oil burning in 1920 and returned to the Bibby Line services. In 1939 she was again converted to a hospital ship and was initially based at Freetown, and later in the Mediterranean and the Far East. She repatriated the wounded from Hong Kong in 1945 and brought wounded servicemen back to the United Kingdom from the Far East the following year. This was followed by a voyage from Palestine with troops in 1948 and a voyage with pilgrims to Jeddah. She was trooping from Trieste to Port Said in 1950 and was sold to the Pan Islamic Steamship Company and renamed *Safina el Arab* in 1951. *Oxfordshire* was broken up in 1958.

The Pacific Steam Navigation Company's *Reina del Pacifico* was built in 1931 for the South American service. In 1932 she recommenced the 'Round South America' service, which became an annual sailing. She served as a troopship during the Second World War and carried King Peter of Yugoslavia from Liverpool to Suez in August 1945. She was returned to her builders in 1947 to be converted back to a passenger liner. However, on trials an engine-room explosion killed twenty-eight men when the piston overheated. She was back on her owner's Liverpool–Valparaiso service in 1948 and went aground at Bermuda in July 1957. She lost a propeller at Havana later that year but survived until 1958 when she was sold and broken up at Newport.

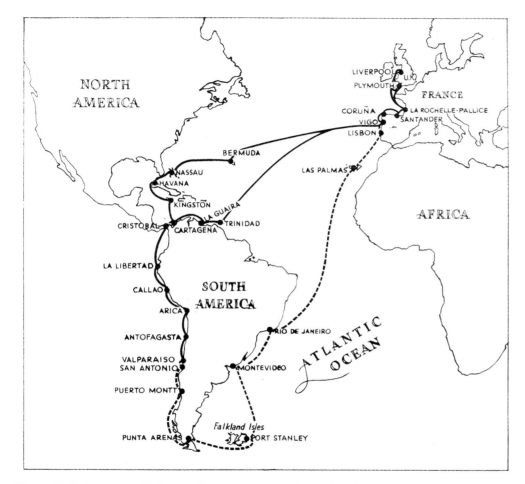

Above left: Pacific Steam Navigation Company routes to South America.

Above right: Ebro and *Essequibo* advert for voyages from New York to Peru and Chile. *Ebro* left New York on 24 January 1923 on a sixty-eight-day cruise around South America.

Above and below: City of Nagpur was built in 1922 for Ellerman City Line. She was the first 'City' liner to exceed 10,000 tons and was placed on the line's Bombay, and later Japan, routes. She was laid up at Bombay in 1933 and operated to South Africa the following year. *City of Nagpur* carried out a series of cruises to the Norwegian fjords and northern capitals from 1936 to 1939. On 24 April 1941 she was torpedoed by U-75 west of Fastnet with 300 passengers and 215 of her crew on board. One passenger and ten of her crew lost their lives.

Right: Ellerman's City & Hall Lines *City of Cairo* one-class cabin service list of fares, 1932.

ELLERMAN'S
CITY & HALL LINES
s.s. "CITY OF CAIRO"—One Class Cabin Service
LIST OF FARES

| | Between U.K. and | | | | | | | |
| | Bombay or Karachi | | Colombo | | Madras | | Calcutta | |
	Single	Return	Single	Return	Single	Return	Single	Retur
	£	£	£	£	£	£	£	£
PROMENADE DECK								
Two Berth Cabins								
Nos. 1 and 6 - per Berth	46	80	47	82	49	86	51	89
Three Berth Cabins								
Nos. 2, 3, 4, 5 ,,	42	73	43	75	45	79	47	82
BRIDGE DECK								
Single Berth Cabins								
Nos. 14, 16, 39 per Cabin	50	87	51	89	53	93	55	96
Bedstead Cabins								
Nos. 8, 10, 11, 12 per Berth	49	86	50	87	52	91	54	94
Two Berth Cabins								
Nos. 18, 20, 22, 25, 29, 30, 32, 34, 36 ,,	44	77	45	79	47	82	49	86
Nos. 7, 9, 24, 28 ,,	46	80	47	82	49	86	51	89
Three Berth Cabins								
Nos. 12a, 15, 17, 19, 21, 23, 31, 33, 35, 37, 38 ,,	41	72	41	72	43	75	45	79
Nos. 26 and 27 ,,	40	70	40	70	42	73	44	77
UPPER DECK (Forward)								
Single Berth Cabins								
Nos. 53 and 55 per Cabin	48	84	49	86	51	89	53	93
Nos. 48 and 54 ,,	50	87	51	89	53	93	55	96
Bedstead Rooms with Bath								
Nos. 46 and 47 per Berth	60	105	61	107	63	110	65	114
Two Berth Cabins								
Nos. 43 and 45 ,,	43	75	44	77	46	80	48	84
Nos. 51 and 52 ,,	44	77	45	79	47	82	49	86
Three Berth Cabins								
Nos. 44, 49, 50 ,,	41	72	41	72	43	75	45	79
UPPER DECK (Aft)								
Two Berth Cabins								
Nos. 59, 61, 63, 65, 66, 68 ,,	39	68	40	70	42	73	44	77
Nos. 56, 57, 71, 72 ,,	37	65	38	66	40	70	42	73
Three Berth Cabins								
Nos. 58, 60, 62, 64, 67, 69, 70 ,,	37	65	38	66	40	70	42	73

Fares between MARSEILLES and BOMBAY or KARACHI are **£3** Single and **£5** Return less in each case

Children will be charged as follows:—3 years of age and under 12 years, Half-fare each; One Child under 3, with parents, Free (no berth provided); Each additional Child under 3 years, One quarter of the Adult Rate. Children of 12 years or over, Full Fare.

European Servants accompanying employers are charged minimum Cabin Class Fares.

Allowances:—Cabin Class Fares are subject to the Companies usual Rebooking Allowances, and Families, Teaplanters, Railway Employees, Missionaries, etc., are granted the customary abatements. Full particulars are given in Companies' Handbooks.

Frank's '50th Anniversary Cruise de Luxe' Mediterranean cruise by *Scythia* on 29 January 1925. *Scythia* was built in 1921 for Cunard's Liverpool–New York service. She was the first of five 'S' class vessels and was completed at Lorient because of an industrial dispute at her builders. In 1928 she accommodated King Amanulla of Afghanistan at Prince's Landing Stage while he was on a visit to Liverpool and took Americans to Cardiff for the Welsh Eisteddfod. In 1939 she became a troopship and was damaged at Algiers by torpedo on 23 November 1942. She sank at the berth and later sailed to Gibraltar and New York to be repaired. She was chartered in 1948 to take people from Germany to Canada and then returned to John Brown's yard on the Clyde to be refitted. *Scythia* returned to commercial service in 1950 and was broken up at Inverkeithing in 1958.

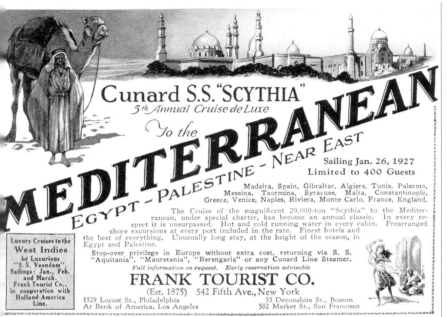

Above, left: 1927 Mediterranean cruise by *Scythia* on 26 January 1927. *Saxonia* was delivered in 1900 for the Boston service. On 8 July 1914 she made the first call by a Cunard liner at Patras and from 1914 to 1915 she was used as a German prisoner of war vessel on the River Thames. Later in the war she carried out trooping duties, returning to commercial service on the London–New York route in 1918. She was sold and broken up in 1925.

Above, right: Cunard's *Mauretania* in white at Madeira while cruising in 1933.

Left: Saxonia

Above: Yoma was built in 1928 for Henderson Line. In February 1941 she transported civilians from the Dutch East Indies to Darwin when Japanese troops took over the country. She was torpedoed twice on 17 June 1943 in convoy in the Mediterranean and sank within five minutes. *Yoma* was on a voyage to Sicily to assist in the landings with around 1,500 troops on board. 800 troops were rescued but over 500 lost their lives.

Left: 133-day world cruise from New York by *Empress of Australia,* sailing from New York on 2 December 1927.

The Henderson Liner *Burma* arrives at her berth in Birkenhead to load cargo for Rangoon. She was built in 1914 by William Denny & Brothers at Dumbarton. *Burma* operated as a troopship during the Second World War and on 27 December 1943 she grounded near Mombasa. She was floated the following April and was sold in 1949 and renamed *Florentia*. Purchased by the Pan Islamic Steam Ship Company in 1953, she was renamed *Safina E Nusrat*. She was broken up in 1957.

Demerara was built in 1912 for the Royal Mail Lines service from Liverpool to the River Plate. In February 1916 she was involved in an incident with the German raider *Moewe* in the South Atlantic but the German vessel did not attack her. On 1 July the following year she was torpedoed off La Rochelle and again survived and was able to reach port. She was broken up in 1933 in Japan.

AUTUMN
BY CRUISES
ROYAL MAIL
TO THE
MEDITERRANEAN
By R.M.S.P. Arcadian and Araguaya
SEPT. 13   OCT. 4
INCLUDING VISITS TO NAPLES,
ATHENS, CONSTANTINOPLE AND
ALGIERS

Special Cruise by M.V. Alcantara
TO THE WEST INDIES
17 JANUARY, 1930

Apply
THE ROYAL MAIL STEAM PACKET CO.,
America House, Cockspur Street, S.W.1.
Telephone: Regent 4975. Royal Mail House,
Leadenhall Street, E.C.3.   Telephone: Royal
9120.   Southampton, Liverpool, Birmingham,
Manchester, Cardiff, Glasgow or Local Agents.

'ATLANTIS'
Spring and Summer Cruises to Mediterranean, North and West Africa, Northern Capitals, Norwegian Fjords, Iceland, Spitzbergen, etc.
7 to 23 Days

'ASTURIAS'
Summer Cruises by the luxurious turbine steamer 'ASTURIAS' to Spain, Portugal, Norway, Mediterranean, etc.   **6 to 14 Days**

Please write for full particulars of these and other 'ATLANTIS' and 'ASTURIAS' Cruises.

ROYAL MAIL
FOR CRUISING AT ITS BEST
ROYAL MAIL LINES LTD., America House, Cockspur Street, S.W.1.   Royal Mail House, Leadenhall Street, E.C.3.   Southampton, Liverpool, Birmingham, Glasgow, Cardiff or Local Agents.

Above: Royal Mail's *Atlantis* at Malta.

Far left: *Arcadian* and *Araguaya* advert 1930.

Left: *Atlantis* and *Asturias* advertisement.

Below: The Royal Mail vessel *Highland Monarch* at Vigo.

City of Benares was built in 1936 for Ellerman Lines as the only two-funnelled ship ever to be built for them. She was chartered by the Ministry of Shipping for a Liverpool–Montreal voyage in 1940 under the Government's Children's Overseas Evacuation Board. She sailed from Liverpool on 13 September with 406 on board and was the commodore ship of a nineteen-ship convoy. The escorting warships left the convoy on 17 September and later that day City of Benares was torpedoed. Lifeboats were launched and City of Benares sank within forty minutes. There was a loss of 248 lives and the 145 survived the sinking were rescued by HMS Hurricane and HMS Anthony.

A White Star liner embarks passengers at Liverpool landing stage.

The White Star liner *Georgic* in Gladstone Dock, Liverpool. She was delivered in 1932 as the final vessel built for the White Star Line. *Georgic* and her sister *Britannic* completed a number of cruises from New York in the 1930s. In 1939 she was requisitioned by the Admiralty as a troopship and was converted to carry 3,000 servicemen. In March 1940 she helped to evacuate British troops from Norway and France before sailing to the Middle East and completing two Atlantic crossings. She arrived at Port Tewfik on 7 July 1941 and was bombed by German aircraft and set on fire. She was beached on 16 July and it was decided that she should be salvaged. Water was pumped out of her hull by a salvage vessel and she was towed to Port Sudan by *City of Sydney* and *Clan Campbell*. She was then towed to Karachi and dry-docked at Bombay. She left Bombay on 20 January 1943, arriving at Liverpool on 1 March, and was then sent to Belfast to be repaired. These repairs were completed by December the following year and she was then owned by the Ministry of War Transport, with Cunard-White Star as managers. In 1945–46 she was employed trooping to Italy, the Middle East and India. She was refitted in 1948 for the Australian emigrant service and was chartered by Cunard in 1950 for the Liverpool–New York service, and the following year for the Southampton–New York route. The charter was repeated for the next three years. She carried out a trooping voyage in 1955 and was chartered to the Australian Government. She was laid up and sold to be broken up in 1956 at Faslane.

On board the *Strathnaver*

Above: *Britannic* in the Mersey berthing at Liverpool landing stage. She was also built by Harland & Wolff at Belfast and sailed on her maiden voyage from Liverpool to New York on 28 June 1930. In the winter season she carried out cruises to the West Indies from New York. *Britannic* was also converted to a troopship at the outbreak of the Second World War and returned to commercial service in March 1947. In 1948 she was employed on the Liverpool–New York service with cruises from New York to the Caribbean during the winter months. On 25 November 1960 she left New York for Liverpool on the last passenger sailing by a White Star vessel. On arrival she was sold and broken up at Inverkeithing.

Right and below: April 1932 P&O Cruises advert.

NO MATTER WHAT YOU THINK OR SAY
WE MUST GO BACK—JUST THIS ONE DAY

.. uneM ..

liatkcoC eciuJ otamoT   ecalG—noleM
raivaC—ggE
eiraV—servuŒ'd sroH

eroruA emmosnoC   tograM enieR emerC
nitarG ua puoS noinO

ettaverC ecuaS—iadamA dehcaoP
tiabetihW delliveD

ereicnaniF—sdaerbteewS
ettocoC ne noegiP
drogireP—maH fo elabmiT

sekaC otatoP—feeB fo sbiR dna niolriS
selliuoN—laeV fo telliF tsaoR
ecuaS elppA—gnilkcuD

snoinO desiarB   rebmucuC demaerC
saeP neerG hserF
seotatoP nitarG ua dna wonS ,tsaoR ,delioB

eniamoR hcnuP

nosserC—nekcihC aeniuG tsaoR
yreleC   tiurF—sdalaS

: TEFFUB DLOC
noitneM ot suoremuN ooT

: LLIRG EHT MORF
inraG—teltuC bmaL   nekcihC gnirpS

gnidduP mulP   ssecnirP elopaeniP
egnopS eseehC nomeL   itturF ittuT epuoC
sruoF stiteP
suoiraV—secI

tiurF detrossA

ynablA epanaC

eeffoC   aeT

.unem siht daer ot desu eb tonnac srorrim seidaL

Above, left: P&O Cruises by 'Electric Ships' advertisement, March 1932.

Above: Menu from *Franconia*'s 1936 world cruise, as the ship lost a day at the Meridian.

Left: Relaxing on the promenade deck on a P&O cruise.

WORLD CRUISE

1932—greatest of Cruising Years—culminates with Canadian Pacific's magnificent Round the World Cruise, a grand and enthralling pageant of colourful countries and picturesque peoples, by the beautiful new 42,500-ton luxury liner

Empress of Britain

the Cruise-Ship Supreme—Biggest ever to encircle the globe.

Designed and built for ultra-luxury Cruising (decorated by Artists of international fame, equipped in the most modern manner, and unrivalled in Service and Cuisine), the great white Empress will follow an itinerary carefully planned to visit the various countries at the best time of year for each. Thus you are in the Holy Land at Christmas, Cairo on New Year's Eve, India in the Cool Season, Japan in Blossom time and dozens of other interesting places when things are at their best. Make your decision now, and book at once for this event of a lifetime!

Duration   -   Four to five months

From Southampton	-	November 23
From New York	-	December 3
From Monaco	-	December 16

rite for
al World
se Bro-
e, to A. D.
ell, Cruise
Dept.

ANADIAN PACIFIC

rld's
eatest
vel

62-65 Charing Cross, London, S.W.1 ; 103 Leadenhall Street, London, E.C.3, or Local Agents

---

WEST INDIES Cruise

There's hidden treasure on the Spanish Main where the buccaneers of old matched cunning and skill with trim merchantmen for a booty of doubloons !

There's treasure, too, in the warm sea air and inviting charm in the sun-kissed Islands of the Caribbean. Plan now to escape winter's chill and visit the Island Paradise of the West Indies on the beautiful modern 20,000-ton cruise-ship

DUCHESS OF RICHMOND

This famous ship is the last word in travel comfort. The cabins have beds (instead of bunks) running hot and cold water, capacious wardrobes, and private bathrooms if desired. The Public Rooms are spacious and exquisitely furnished. There are wide Games Decks, a Gymnasium, and an outdoor Sunbathing Pool. WARM SOUTHERLY ROUTE out via Gibraltar and home via Madeira. Intinerary includes : Trinidad, Venezuela, Curaçao, Panama, Jamaica, Cuba, Bahamas, Porto Rico, Barbados, Grenada, and St. Lucia.

From SOUTHAMPTON, JAN. 28, 1933

FIRST CLASS ONLY — LIMITED MEMBERSHIP

MINIMUM RATE : 80 Gns.

ROUND THE WORLD CRUISE
BY THE EMPIRE SHIP, the magnificent 42,500-ton
EMPRESS OF BRITAIN
Specially planned itinerary, visiting the World's most attractive countries, each at the best time of the year. From SOUTHAMPTON, November 23. Fares from 359 gns. (exclusive of shore excursions). From MONACO, December 16. Fares from 325 gns. (exclusive of shore excursions).
Write for Special World Cruise Brochure.

Full information and Cabin Plans on application to A. D. Powell, Cruise Dept.

CANADIAN PACIFIC

World's Greatest Travel System.

62-65 Charing Cross, Trafalgar Sq., London, S.W.1, 103 Leadenhall Street, London, E.C.3, or Local Agents Everywhere.

ROYAL MAIL

CRUISE ROUND AFRICA

BY "ATLANTIS"

FROM SOUTHAMPTON
3RD FEBRUARY 1933

57 DAYS 135 GUINEAS AND UPWARDS

ALSO CHRISTMAS CRUISE TO THE

MEDITERRANEAN

21 DEC. 1932 17 DAYS FROM 20 GUINEAS

CHRISTMAS WEEK-END CRUISE BY

"ASTURIAS"

23-27 DEC. FROM 8 GNS.

FOR ILLUSTRATED BROCHURE APPLY

ROYAL MAIL LINES, LTD.

AMERICA HOUSE, COCKSPUR STREET, S.W.1. ROYAL MAIL HOUSE, LEADENHALL ST., E.C.3. SOUTHAMPTON, LIVERPOOL, BIRMINGHAM, MANCHESTER, CARDIFF, GLASGOW, OR LOCAL AGENTS

SUNBATHE IN WINTER!

SPECIAL XMAS & NEW YEAR TOURS to SOUTH AFRICA

at reduced return fares

1st Class	-	£90
2nd Class	-	£60
3rd Class	-	£30

Write for illustrated folder Head Office, 3, Fenchurch Street, London, E.C.3.

West End Agency, 125, Pall Mall, S.W.1

UNION CASTLE LINE

Far left: Empress of Britain world cruise, 1932.

Left: Duchess of Richmond cruise from Southampton on 28 January 1933.

Above left: Round Africa Cruise on Atlantis, 1933.

Above right: Union Castle advert 1932.

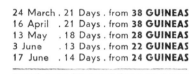

George-
nother
'ATLANTIS' special—

Sunshine, Scenery, Luxury, Laughter—just a suspicion
of Laziness and a dash of Jazz—These are the
ingredients of the finest "pick-me-up" you can have;
a speciality aboard the wonder cruising ship "Atlantis."

SPRING CRUISES TO THE MEDITERRANEAN

13 MAY . . . . 18 DAYS from **28** GUINEAS
3 JUNE . . . . 13 DAYS from **22** GUINEAS
17 JUNE . . . . 14 DAYS from **24** GUINEAS

NORTHERN CAPITALS NORWAY, ICELAND, ETC.

2 JULY . . . . 12 DAYS from **19** GUINEAS
15 JULY . . . . 7 DAYS from **11** GUINEAS
23 JULY . . . . 19 DAYS from **30** GUINEAS
12 AUG. . . . . . . 22 DAYS from **34** GUINEAS

The Royal Mail Steam Packet Co., London, America House, Cockspur Street, S.W.1,
Royal Mail House, Leadenhall Street, E.C.3, Southampton, Liverpool, Birmingham,
Manchester, Cardiff, Glasgow or Local Agents.

ROYAL MAIL

Come and find summer with us on the

'ATLANTIS'

SPRING CRUISES TO THE MEDITERRANEAN

24 March . 21 Days . from **38** GUINEAS
16 April . 21 Days . from **38** GUINEAS
13 May . 18 Days . from **28** GUINEAS
3 June . 13 Days . from **22** GUINEAS
17 June . 14 Days . from **24** GUINEAS

Special *Easter* Week-end Cruise by Luxury
Motor Liner "ALCANTARA" (23,000 tons) 5 days
from 8 Gns.
Also *Whitsuntide* Week-end Cruise by
"ALMANZORA" 4 days from 7 Gns., and
August Bank Holiday Cruise by "ALCANTARA",
5 days from 8 Gns.

ROYAL MAIL

THE ROYAL MAIL STEAM PACKET CO.
London : America House, Cockspur St., S.W.1
Royal Mail House, Leadenhall Street, E.C.3.
Southampton, Liverpool, Birmingham, Man-
chester, Cardiff, Glasgow or Local Agents

Above left and middle: Atlantis, *Alcantara* and *Almanzora* Mediterranean and Northern Capitals cruises 1932.

Above right: A visit to the bridge of a P&O cruise ship.

Laconia and *Franconia* cruises, 1932. *Franconia* was fitted with a swimming pool for her winter cruises from New York. In 1926, when she was cruising in the West Indies, she went aground at San Juan, Puerto Rico. In 1931 she was chartered by Furness Bermuda Line to replace the *Monarch of Bermudai,* which had suffered a serious fire. Two years later her hull was painted white for her world cruise from New York, and her 1938 world cruise took her to thirty-seven ports and covered 41,727 miles. She was refitted as a troopship during the Second World War and was returned to service in 1949. Following a successful cruising programme in 1956 she was sold and broken up at Inverkeithing.

Cunard Winter Cruises

January—April, 1932
'LACONIA' (20,000 tons)
WEST INDIES & WEST AFRIC
From Liverpool, Jan. 22nd
From Plymouth, Jan. 23rd
46 days ... ... from 95 gns
MADEIRA, SPAIN, N. AFRIC
AND MEDITERRANEAN
From Southampton, Mar. 12th
(including the Easter holidays)
21 days ... ... from 42 gns
SPAIN, N. AFRICA, CANARY
ISLES & PORTUGAL
From Southampton, April 5th
16 days ... ... from 32 gns.
'FRANCONIA'
WORLD CRUISE, 1932
From London, Jan. 21st, returning
Plymouth early June
Rates from £375

Write for further particulars to
Cunard Line, Liverpool, London
or local offices and agencies

Homeric and *Laconia* cruises, 1934/35. *Laconia* was built in 1922 and undertook a number of summer cruises from Hamburg and New York the following year. In the 1930s she cruised regularly from the United Kingdom and New York.

These pages: Aberdeen & Commonwealth Line and Canadian Pacific advertisements.

Atlantic Excursions

NEW RATES AT SINGLE FARE & A THIRD

The special Cunard White Star excursions and new fares make it easy and convenient to visit your friends and relatives in America during the winter months. Fifteen days are allowed on the other side, and the new rates apply in either direction. Moreover you are assured of supreme travel comfort and a novel and exhilarating holiday,

SPEND EASTER WITH YOUR FRIENDS AND RELATIVES OVERSEAS

TOURIST AND THIRD CLASS

from . . £21 15s.

according to class and steamer.

*Write for special leaflet to
Cunard White Star Limited, London, Liverpool
or local offices and agents.*

Cunard White Star

Christmas Winter & Spring Cruises, 1934-1935

Sailing Date 1934	Vessel	From	Ports of Call	No. of Days	Rates from
Dec. 21	HOMERIC *Christmas Cruise*	Southampton	Lisbon, Las Palmas, Cruising in the Tropics Teneriffe, Madeira.	15	26 Gns.
*Dec. 29	FRANCONIA * (Passengers may also sail from Southampton in the Majestic, Jan. 2nd, joining the Franconia at New York.)	Southampton	World Cruise. Across Southern Hemisphere visiting:— South Sea Isles, New Zealand, Australia, Bali, Java, Singapore, Penang, Madras, Ceylon, Seychelles, Madagascar, East and South Africa, South America and home via New York.	153	395 Gns. Including standard shore excursions and Atlantic crossings.
1935 Jan. 26	HOMERIC	Southampton	Teneriffe, Martinique, Haiti, Nassau, Havana, Kingston, Cristobal, Curacao, Venezuela, Trinidad, Grenada, Barbados, Madeira.	45	90 Gns.
Feb. 6	LACONIA	Liverpool	Lisbon, Palma, Malta, Alexandria, Haifa, Larnaca, Rhodes, Istanbul, Athens, Messina, Naples, Monaco, Barcelona, Gibraltar.	35	55 Gns.
Mar. 16	HOMERIC	Southampton	Palma, Monaco, Naples, Athens, Rhodes, Haifa, Port Said, Messina, Monaco, Gibraltar.	28	48 Gns.
Apl. 18	HOMERIC *(Easter Cruise)*	Southampton	Monaco, Naples, Palermo, Algiers, Lisbon.	16	28 Gns.

FIRST CLASS PASSENGERS ONLY

Cunard White Star

Fuller information can be obtained from any Cunard White Star office or agent.

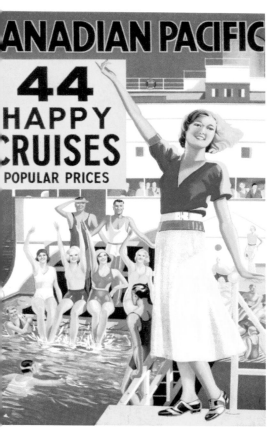

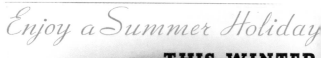

Typical advertisements for cruises in the 1930s.

Above left: P&O cruise advert.

Above right: P&O spring and summer cruises, 1934.

Right: Viceroy of India cruises, 1936. She was built in 1929 for the London–India service and was also employed cruising in the 1930s. A swimming pool was fitted in 1938. However, she was converted to a troopship in 1940, and on 11 November 1942 she was torpedoed by U-407 off Oran, Algeria, and four troops on board lost their lives when she sank.

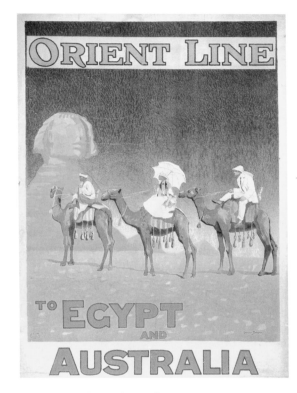

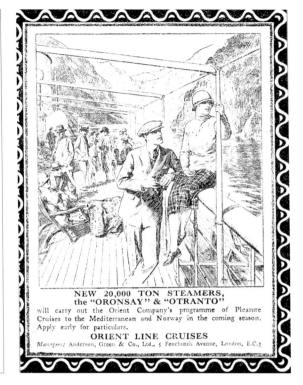

Orient Line adverts for Mediterranean, Norwegian Fjords, Northern Capitals and voyages to Egypt and Australia.

Above: Avelona Star was built as *Avelona* for the Blue Star Line in 1926 with accommodation for 162 first-class passengers, and became *Avelona Star* in 1930. In 1931 she was converted to a cargo vessel and all the passenger accommodation was removed as well as the dummy aft funnel. On 30 June 1940, in convoy she was torpedoed by U-43 and sank the following day. Her crew were picked up by *Beignon*, which was later torpedoed by U-30. The crews of both ships were rescued by HMS *Vesper* and HMS *Windsor*. Three of *Avelona Star*'s crew lost their lives.

Below: The Cunard liner *Alaunia* was built by John Brown & Company at Clydebank in 1925 for the company's Canadian service. In 1933 she made a series of weekend cruises from Liverpool to London at a cost of £4. She was converted to an Armed Merchant Cruiser at the beginning of the Second World War and became a Heavy Repair Ship in 1944, and later a Depot Ship. She was broken up at Blyth in 1957.

Right: 1935 Cunard White Star advert for *Homeric, Laconia, Lancastria, Doric* and *Laurentic*.

SEA AND SUN-BATHING AT THE "HOMERIC'S" LIDO

Come Cruising !

No matter at what time of the year—spring, summer autumn or winter—you will always be able to find a Cunard White Star cruise to suit. Between Christmas and next autumn there is a choice of thirty delightful cruises to colourful ports in the Mediterranean, West Indies, Atlantic Isles and Norway by the magnificent cruising liners "Homeric," "Laconia," "Lancastria" "Doric" and "Laurentic"

From £7 One Class Only

Full details of the itineraries will be found in the booklet

Cunard White Star

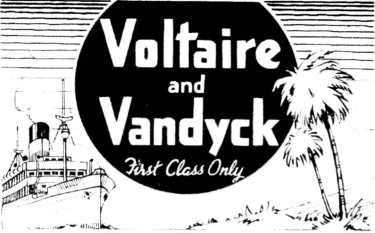

Voltaire and Vandyck

First Class Only

Window or porthole in every room.

EASTER CRUISES

APRIL 14. "VOLTAIRE" from Southampton to Canary Islands, calling at Casablanca, Santa Cruz de la Palma, Las Palmas, Teneriffe, Madeira and Lisbon. **18 Days from 25 Gns.**

APRIL 14. "VANDYCK" from Liverpool to the Mediterranean, calling at Gibraltar, Villefranche, (Monte Carlo, Nice), Naples, Capri and Lisbon. **19 Days from 26 Gns.**

MAY CRUISES

MAY 7. "VOLTAIRE" from Southampton to the Dalmatian Coast and Venice, calling at Palermo, Kotor, Dubrovnik, Venice, Abbazia, Corfu, Malta and Lisbon. **24 Days from 34 Gns.**

MAY 14. "VANDYCK" from Liverpool to Atlantic Islands, calling at Santa Cruz de la Palma, Madeira and Lisbon. **14 Days from 18 Gns.**

WHITSUN CRUISES

JUNE 4. "VOLTAIRE" from Southampton to the Mediterranean, calling at Gibraltar, Villefranche, (Monte Carlo, Nice), Naples, Capri and Lisbon. **18 Days from 25 Gns.**

JUNE 4. "VANDYCK" from Liverpool to Atlantic Islands and Morocco, calling at Madeira, Casablanca and Lisbon. **13 Days from 17 Gns**

For full details of above apply:

LAMPORT & HOLT LINE LTD.

ROYAL LIVER BUILDING, LIVERPOOL 3 - - (Tel.: Bank 8850). 27 LEADENHALL STREET, LONDON E.C.3 (Tel.: Royal 5723). 64 CROSS STREET

Voltaire and *Vandyck* advertisements for 1935 cruises.

LAMPORT & HOLT CRUISES

T.S.S. VOLTAIRE and VANDYCK

FIRST CLASS ONLY

Windows or Portholes in every room.

CHRISTMAS CRUISE

T.S.S. "VOLTAIRE" from SOUTHAMPTON

December 21. Saturday.

Calling at Lisbon, Casablanca, Teneriffe, Madeira **15 days from 20 gns**

TO HOLY LAND AND EGYPT

T.S.S. "VOLTAIRE" from SOUTHAMPTON

February 1. Saturday. **33 days from 42 gns**

March 7. Saturday. **30 ,, ,, 38 ,,**

CRUISE TO WEST INDIES

T.S.S. "VANDYCK" from SOUTHAMPTON

February 15. Saturday.

Madeira, Barbados (Bridgetown), Trinidad (Port of Spain), Panama (Cristobal), Jamaica (Kingston), Cuba (Havana), Florida (Miami), Bahamas (Nassau), Bermuda, Azores (Ponta Delgada) .. .. .. **48 days from 70 gns**

LAMPORT & HOLT LINE Ltd.

Royal Liver Building, LIVERPOOL.
27 & 98 Leadenhall Street, London, E.C.3.

Tel. Add.—"Lamport," L'pool.   Tel. Add.—"Lamport," Fen London

Left and below: Voltaire was delivered to the Lamport & Holt Line in 1923 for the Liverpool–New York–South America service. She was laid up in 1930 and began cruising with a white hull two years later. *Voltaire* and her sister *Vandyck* were very successful cruising ships in the 1930s. She carried out trooping duties at the beginning of the Second World War and was later used as an accommodation ship to HMS *Royal Oak* and HMS *Iron Duke*. In 1939 she was converted to an Armed Merchant Cruiser, becoming HMS *Voltaire*. She was in Malta in 1940 working as a contraband and inspection vessel and later acted as a North Atlantic convoy escort vessel. On 4 April 1941 she was attacked by the German auxiliary cruiser *Thor*. She sank with a loss of life of 75, and 197 survivors were taken aboard the *Thor*.

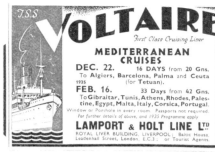

Voltaire and *Vandyck* cruises, 1935.

P&O liners at Sydney, Australia.

Modasa was built for the British India Line in 1921 for their service to India and East Africa. She operated as a cargo vessel for most of the Second World War and following her overhaul in 1946 carried 183 passengers in one class. She survived until 1954 when she was sold to be broken up at Blyth.

The British India passenger and cargo vessel *Aronda* was built in 1912. She carried out various trooping duties during the First World War and was sold in 1932 and broken up at Bombay.

The second *Aronda* in the fleet was completed in 1941 and the following year she transported servicemen of the 6th Australian Division from Australia to Colombo. At the end of the war she operated on the company's Bombay–Durban service carrying forty-four first-class, twenty-two second-class and twenty-eight interchangeable passengers. She was later transferred to the Karachi–Chittagong route and was sold in 1963 to be broken up at Hong Kong.

Left and below: Coast Lines' *Killarney* and later *Lady Killarney* undertook cruises around the British Isles. *Lady Killarney* was built by Harland & Wolff in 1912 as *Lady Leinster*, becoming *Lady Connaught* in 1938. She was seriously damaged by mines in 1940 but was converted to a livestock carrier two years later and a hospital ship in 1944. Following the end of hostilities it was decided that Coast Lines would continue their programme of cruises and she was converted to carry passengers by Harland & Wolff in 1946–47, and renamed *Lady Killarney*. She was sold and broken up at Port Glasgow in 1956.

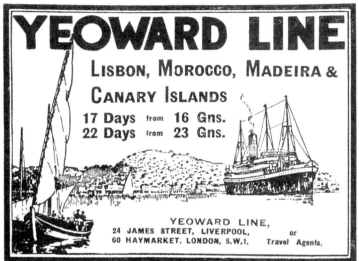

Left and below: Yeoward Line cruise ship *Alondra.* The Yeoward Line was managed by Yeoward Brothers and *Alondra* inaugurated their passenger and cargo service from Liverpool to Lisbon, Madeira and the Canary Islands in 1899. The three-week cruise on *Alondra* in 1922 allowed a stay of three days in Lisbon, one day in Madeira and five days in the Canary Islands to load her cargo of bananas for the United Kingdom.

The cargo and passenger vessel *Hilary* was built in 1931 by Cammell Laird & Company Limited at Birkenhead for Booth Lines' service from Liverpool to Manaus. The voyage was advertised as 'The Forest Tour, 1,000 miles up the Mighty Amazon' via Oporto, Lisbon and Madeira. *Hilary* operated on the route until 1959 when she was sold and broken up at Inverkeithing.

This page and opposite page: Empress of Britain made a fabulous world cruise every year.from Southampton and New York.

CANADIAN PACIFIC CRUISES

Jolliest under the Sun!

Gay Holiday Cruises by Famous Atlantic Liners equipped for your personal comfort. Glorious Sunshine, Healthy Sea Air, Fun and Good Companionship.

Itineraries planned to interest, instruct and amuse. Cruises for everybody, five days to four and a half months duration. Prices to suit all purses.

Mediterranean	Atlantic Isles
Norwegian Fjords	West Indies

Round the World

Gloucestershire was built in 1910 and was the sister of *Leicestershire*. On 11 July 1913 she represented Bibby Line at the Mersey Pageant, and two years later she was converted to an Armed Merchant Cruiser as HMS *Gloucestershire* for service with the 10th Cruiser Squadron. In 1917 she was engaged in trooping duties prior to returning to commercial service on the Birkenhead–Rangoon route. She was broken up at Pembroke Dock in 1936.

Opposite, left: Timetable for winter cruises, Furness Bermuda.
Right, Boat deck on *Monarch of Bermuda*.

FURNESS
BERMUDA
LINE
WINTER
Rates and Sailings

EFFECTIVE
Feb. 2nd, 1939

S.S. MONARCH OF BERMUDA
S.S. QUEEN OF BERMUDA

Monarch of Bermuda and *Queen of Bermuda,* courtesy Stephen Card.

P&O Line's *Corfu* in London Docks. She was delivered in 1931 for the Far East services, became an Armed Merchant Cruiser during the Second World War and later carried out trooping duties. She returned to P&O in 1949 and was broken up in 1961.

Above: Carthage was built in 1931 for P&O's Far East service and was placed on the Australian run the following year. She operated as an Armed Merchant Cruiser from 1939 to 1943 and as a troopship for the rest of the war. She returned to commercial service in 1948 and was broken up in 1961.

Right: Canton was built by Alexander Stephen & Sons in 1938 for P&O's London–Suez–Far East service. She operated as an Armed Merchant Cruiser and troopship during the Second World War, returning to service in 1946. She was broken up in 1962.

Atlantis sunshine cruises, 1936. *Atlantis* was originally intended to be built for the Pacific Steam Navigation Company but was transferred on the stocks to the Royal Mail Line and named *Andes*. Her maiden voyage took her from Liverpool to Valparaiso, and at the outbreak of the First World War she was converted to an Armed Merchant Cruiser. She returned to commercial service in 1919 and was converted to a cruise liner in 1929 at Liverpool. She was renamed *Atlantis*, painted white and fitted with a swimming pool behind the bridge. In 1939, she became a hospital ship and was later used to repatriate prisoners of war. In 1948 she was chartered to carry emigrants to Australia and New Zealand from the United Kingdom and was broken up at Faslane in 1952.

The Royal Mail Lines passenger vessel *Asturias* operated on the company's Southampton–River Plate service but also made several voyages to New York and undertook a number of cruises out of the United Kingdom.

Above: Scythia.

Right: United Baltic Corporation Limited poster, 1936.

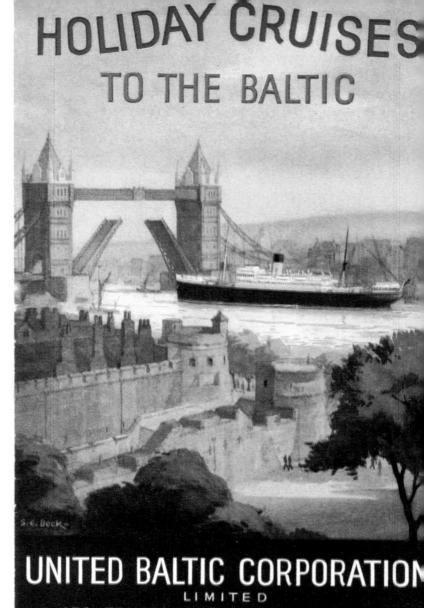

HOLIDAY CRUISES
TO THE BALTIC

S.C. Beck

UNITED BALTIC CORPORATION
LIMITED

HENDERSON LINE

WINTER FARES.

Regular Passenger Services

Gibraltar	-	£14 return
Palma	-	£17 return
Marseilles	-	£18 return
Port Said	-	£43 return
Port Sudan	-	£53 return
Rangoon	-	£86 return

For full particulars apply

P. HENDERSON & CO.

95,
Bothwell Street,
GLASGOW, C.2.
or
7 Billiter Square,
LONDON, E.C.3.
Royal Liver
Building,
LIVERPOOL.

Royal Mail & Pacific Lines
TO SOUTH AMERICA

PASSENGER AND FREIGHT SERVICES
To BRAZIL, URUGUAY & ARGENTINA,
From Southampton, London and Liverpool.

Tours to Spain, Portugal, Madeira & Canary Islands

From LIVERPOOL to BERMUDA, BAHAMAS,
HAVANA, PANAMA, PERU, CHILE.

Tours to Bermuda and Bahamas inclusive of Hotel.

ROYAL MAIL LINES, LTD.
THE PACIFIC STEAM NAVIGATION COMPANY.

London: America House, Cockspur Street, S.W.1., Royal Mail House,
Leadenhall Street, E.C.3. Liverpool: Goree, Water Street, Glasgow,
Birmingham, Southampton, Manchester, Cardiff or Local Agents.

Left: 1935 advertisements.

Right: 1936 Canadian Pacific and P&O adverts.

For Your 1936 HOLIDAYS
CANADIAN PACIFIC CRUISES & TOURS

Your Choice of

Try a Canadian Pacific CRUISE or TOUR overseas—the new, fashionable holiday mode that provides the maximum pleasure for people with limited leisure. The Canadian Pacific cruising fleet this year includes: S.S. "EMPRESS OF AUSTRALIA" the famous 22,000 ton "Dreamship of Cruises." First-class only. Limited Membership.

S.S. "DUCHESS OF ATHOLL." S.S. "DUCHESS OF RICHMOND." Splendid modern 20,000 ton cruising liners. First-class only. Limited Membership. S.S. "MONTCALM," "MONCLARE" and "MONTROSE." Popular 16-400 ton liners specially equipped for cruising. One class only. Fares from £1 per day.

- ALGERIA
- CANADA
- CANARY ISLES
- DENMARK
- FINLAND
- FRENCH RIVIERA
- GERMANY
- GREECE
- MOROCCO
- NORWAY
- PORTUGAL
- SENEGAL
- SIERRA LEONE
- SPAIN
- SWEDEN
- TUNISIA
- TURKEY
- U·S·A·
- U·S·S·R·

SHORT TOURS TO CANADA & U.S.A.

Let us help you to plan a New-World Holiday, or join one of our accompanied Short Tours (18 to 32 days), leaving nearly every week from early April to late September. Itineraries include:— **Quebec, Montreal, Ottawa, Niagara Falls, French River, New York, Chicago,** etc. Special "all-in" fares cover complete cost, including the Atlantic crossing both ways by the short sea route with a splendid 1,000 miles smooth-water cruise through the picturesque St. Lawrence seaway.

2 GRAND TOURS ACROSS CANADA

We have also two grand tours across **Canada** this season, each of seven weeks duration, traversing the Dominion, from Atlantic to Pacific and visiting all the principal cities, town and beauty spots, one tour leaving May 29th and the other July 24th. "All-in" fares cover everything. Write for our 1936 Programme.

CANADIAN PACIFIC.

62-65 Charing Cross (Trafalgar Square), London, S.W.1.
103 Leadenhall Street, London, E.C.3; or Local Agents everywhere.

WORLD'S GREATEST TRAVEL SYSTEM

FIVE FINE SHIPS

1936 CRUISING?

Yes . . . and we shall go by P. & O. . . . for their cruising programme is always attractive. Five fine ships. A choice of nineteen cruises. Norway. The Mediterranean. The Northern Capitals. Madeira. A cruise to suit practically every purse. You can travel first-class and remain first-class. Travel tourist and feel first-class . . . For whatever you pay you will have a first-class time if you cruise by

14 COCKSPUR ST., S.W.1; 130 LEADEN-HALL ST., E.C.3; AUSTRALIA HOUSE, W.C.2; or Local Agents.

FIRST CLASS CRUISES
S.S. Viceroy of India
20,000 tons.

June 19. 14 days, from 21 gns. London and Leith to North Cape, Murmansk and Norway.

July 4. 14 days, from 21 gns. London and Leith to the Norwegian Fjords and Bergen.

July 31. 14 days, from 21 gns. to the Northern Capitals.

Aug. 15. 13 days, from 21 gns. London to Atlantic Isles and Spain.

Aug. 29. 21 days, from 36 gns. Southampton to Constantinople, Grecian Archipelago and North Africa.

CHOICE OF NINETEEN CRUISES

Date	Steamer	Line	From	Duration days	Fares from	Where
May 1	Lancastria (17,000 tons)	Cunard W. Star	Liverpool	22	24 gns.	Malta, Salonika, Kelia Bay, Instanbul, Gibraltar, Liverpool.
1	Alondra (3,500 tons)	Yeoward	Liverpool	18	19 gns.	Lisbon, Madeira, Las Palmas, Santa Cruz, Liverpool.
2	Montcalm (16,400 tons)	Canadian Pacific	Liverpool	13	£13	Gibraltar, Barcelona, Palma, Lisbon, Liverpool.
2	Orion (24,000 tons)	Orient	Liverpool	20	34 gns.	Algiers, Haifa, Beirut, Haifa, Athens, Gibraltar, Southampton.
2	Voltaire (13,248 tons)	L'port & Holt	Southampton	21	28 gns.	Casablanca, Dakar, Bathurst, Santa Cruz de La Palma, Madeira, S'ton
6	Arandora Star (15,000 tons)	Blue Star	Southampton	23	40 gns.	The Riviera, Greece, Yugo-Slavia, Dalmatian Coast, Venice and Tunisia, Southampton.
8	Avoceta (3,500 tons)	Yeoward	Liverpool	18	19 gns.	Lisbon, Madeira, Las Palmas, Santa Cruz, Liverpool.
8	Atlantis (16,000 tons)	Royal Mail	Southampton	20	34 gns.	Gibraltar, Venice, Dubrovnik, Kotor, Algiers, Southampton.
9	Vandyck (13,248 tons)	L'port & Holt	Liverpool	13	16 gns.	Vigo, Ceuta, Palma, Gibraltar, L'p'l.
9	Moldavia (17,000 tons)	P. & O.	London	14	£14	Ceuta, Tarragona, Barcelona, Palma, Algiers, Corunna, London.
12	Stella Polaris (6,000 tons)	B. & N.	Southampton	13	£19	Le Havre, Lisbon, Madeira, Teneriffe, Las Palmas, Vigo, Calais, Dover.
15	Strathnaver (22,500 tons)	P. & O.	London	21	1st £33 T'ist £20	Gibraltar, Bizerta, Port Said, Beirut, Haifa, Port Said, Malta, Lisbon, Southampton.
15	Aguila (3,500 tons)	Yeoward	Liverpool	19	19 gns.	Lisbon, Madeira, Las Palmas, Santa Cruz, Liverpool.
16	Orontes (20,000 tons)	Orient	Liverpool	21	36 gns.	Philippeville, Dubrovnik, Hvar, Korcula, Kotor, Athens, Safi, Lond'n
16	Montcalm (16,400 tons)	Canadian Pacific	Liverpool	13	£13	Tangier, Tarragona, Barcelona, Palma, Cadiz, Liverpool.
19	Dunluce Castle (8,131 tons)	Union Castle	London	10/11	12 gns.	Antwerp, Rotterdam, Hamburg, London.
19	Hector (11,198 tons)	Blue Funnel	London	6	7 gns. thro'out	Glasgow, via N. and W. Coasts Scotland (with two days at Rotterdam)
23	Orion (24,000 tons)	Orient	Southampton	17	27 gns.	Bizerta, Malta, Nauplia, Athens, Ceuta, London.
23	Alondra (3,500 tons)	Yeoward	Liverpool	22	23 gns.	Lisbon, Madeira, Las Palmas, Santa Cruz, La Palma, Orotava, Las Palmas, Liverpool.
29	Stella Polaris (6,000 tons)	B. & N.	Harwich	17	£24	Canary Islands, Morocco, Spain, Portugal, Harwich
29	Killarney (2,000 tons)	Coast Lines	Liverpool	8	8 gns.	Whitsun Cruise. Scottish Firths and Fjords, Liverpool.
29	Meteor (4,000 tons)	B. & N.	Newcastle	8	£14	Whitsun Cruise. Norwegian Fjords, Denmark, Newcastle.
30	Vandyck (13,248 tons)	L'port & Holt	Liverpool	13	16 gns.	Whitsun Cruise. Gibraltar, Palma, Ceuta, Lisbon, Liverpool.
30	Voltaire (13,248 tons)	L'port & Holt	Southampton	18	24 gns.	Whitsun Cruise. Gibraltar, Casablanca, Santa Cruz de La Palma, Madeira (3 days stay), Lisbon, S'ton
30	Arandora Star (15,000 tons)	Blue Star	Southampton	21	35 gns.	Malta, Greece, Gallipoli, Dardanelles, Turkey, Algeria, Spain, S'pton
30	Staffordshire (15,000 tons)	Bibby	London	7	8/10gns.	Hamburg, Liverpool.
30	Montcalm (16,400 tons)	Canadian Pacific	Liverpool	13	£13	Madeira, Las Palmas, Teneriffe, Lisbon, London.
30	Atlantis (16,000 tons)	Royal Mail	Southampton	14	23 gns.	Whitsun Cruise. Vigo, Ceuta, Barcelona, Cannes, Lisbon, S'hampton.
30	Lancastria (17,000 tons)	Cunard W. Star	Liverpool	14	£17	Lisbon, Palma, Monte Carlo, Gibraltar, Liverpool.
June 2	Montclare (16,400 tons)	Canadian Pacific	Southampton	18	£18	Copenhagen, Leningrad, Helsingfors, Stockholm, Zoppot, Travemunde, Southampton.
5	Calypso (4,000 tons)	Wilson	London	10	£10	Brunsbuttel, Holtenau, Copenhagen, Oslo, Christiansand, London.
5	Avoceta (3,500 tons)	Yeoward	Liverpool	19	20 gns.	Lisbon, Madeira, Santa Cruz, Las Palmas, Orotava, Liverpool.
6	Strathnaver (22,500 tons)	P. & O.	Southampton	14	£22 1st £13 T'ist	Bizerta, Villefranche, Barcelona, Palma, Lisbon, Southampton.
6	Killarney (2,000 tons)	Coast Lines	Liverpool	5	5 gns.	Scottish Firths & Fjords, Liverpool.
6	Meteor (4,000 tons)	B. & N.	Newcastle-on-Tyne	7	£12/10	Norheimsund, Bergen, Gudvangen, Balestrand, Newcastle.
12	Killarney (2,000 tons)	Coast Lines	Liverpool	6	6 gns.	Scottish Firths & Fjords, L'pool.
12	Strathaird (22,500 tons)	P. & O.	London	14	£22 1st £13 T'ist	Corfu, Athens, Malta, Southampton.
13	Montcalm (16,400 tons)	Canadian Pacific	Liverpool	13	£13	Gibraltar, Barcelona, Tangier, Lisbon, Liverpool.
13	Vandyck (13,248 tons)	L'port & Holt	Liverpool	13	16 gns.	Tangier, Casablanca, Madeira, Lisbon, L'pool.
13	Aguila (3,500 tons)	Yeoward	Liverpool	22	23 gns.	Lisbon, Madeira, Las Palmas, Santa Cruz, La Palma, Orotava, Las Palmas, Liverpool.

Date	Steamer	Line	From	Duration days	Fares from	Where
June 13	Oxfordshire (12,500 tons)	Bibby	London	7	8/10gns.	Hamburg, Antwerp, Liverpool, N'castle.
13	Meteor (4,000 tons)	B. & N.	Newcastle-on-Tyne	14	£22	Norwegian Fjords, Bergen, N'castle.
16	Stella Polaris (6,000 tons)	B. & N.	Harwich	14	£27	N'wegian Fjords, Nth. Cape, Ha'wich
16	Dunbar Castle (10,002 tons)	Union Castle	London	10/11	12 gns. thro'out	Antwerp, Rotterdam, Hamburg, London.
19	Killarney (2,000 tons)	Coast Lines	Liverpool	13	13 gns.	Scottish Firths & Fjords, Liverpool.
19	Calypso (4,000 tons)	Wilson	London	10	£10	Brunsbuttel, Holtenau, Copenhagen, Oslo, Christiansand, London.
19	Viceroy of India (20,000 tons)	P. & O.	London	14	21 gns.	Leith, Trondhjem, Murmansk, Nth. Cape, Tromsø, Narvik, Bergen, Leith, London.
20	Atlantis (16,000 tons)	Royal Mail	Southampton	13	22 gns.	Coruna, Casablanca, Las Palmas, Santa Cruz de La Palma, Madeira, Lisbon, Southampton.
20	Voltaire (13,248 tons)	L'port & Holt	Southampton	13	16 gns.	Cadiz, Palma, Ceuta, Lisbon, S'mptn
20	Lancastria (17,000 tons)	Cunard W. Star	Liverpool	13	£16	Gibraltar, Tangier, Tarragona, Barcelona, Palma, Lisbon, Liverpool.
20	Aeneas (10,058 tons)	Blue Funnel	London	6	7 gns.	Glasgow, via N. and W. Coasts Scotland (with 2 days Rotterdam).
26	Alondra (3,500 tons)	Yeoward	Liverpool	19	20 gns.	Lisbon, Madeira, Santa Cruz, Las Palmas, Orotava, Liverpool.
27	Arandora Star (15,000 tons)	Blue Star	Southampton	13	20 gns.	Northern Capitals, Germany, Danzig, Lithuania, Sweden, Denmark, Tilbury.
27	Worcestershire (15,000 tons)	Bibby	London	7	8/10 gns.	Hamburg, Liverpool.
27	Orontes (20,000 tons)	Orient	Immingham	13	20 gns.	Stockholm, Helsingfors, Copenhagen, Oslo, Immingham.
27	Montcalm (16,400 tons)	Canadian Pacific	Liverpool	13	£9	Casablanca, Lisbon, Liverpool.
27	Meteor (4,000 tons)	B. & N.	Newcastle-on-Tyne	14	£22	Norwegian Fjords, Bergen, N'castle.
27	City of Nagpur (10,138 tons)	Wilson	Hull	6	£6	Christiansand, Oslo, Hull.
27	Strathaird (22,500 tons)	P. & O.	Southampton	13	£22 1st £12 t'rist	Bizerta, Malta, Barcelona, Lisbon, Southampton.
27	Vandyck (13,248 tons)	L'port and Holt	Liverpool	13	16 gns.	Norwegian Fjords, Bergen, L'pool.
27	Empress of Australia (22,000 tons)	Canadian Pacific	Southampton	20	36 gns.	Oslo, Zoppot, Stockholm, Leningrad, Helsingfors, Copenhagen, Travemunde, London.
July 1	Stella Polaris (6,000 tons)	B. & N.	Harwich	14	£27	Bergen, Norwegian Fjords, North Cape, Harwich.
3	Killarney (2,000 tons)	Coast Lines	Liverpool	13	13 gns.	Scottish Firths & Fjords, L'pool.
3	Calypso (4,000 tons)	Wilson	London	10	£10	Brunsbuttel, Holtenau, Copenhagen Oslo, Christiansand, London.
3	Moldavia (17,000 tons)	P. & O.	London	14	£14	Malaga, Villefranche, Palma, Lisbon, Southampton.
4	Viceroy of India (20,000 tons)	P. & O.	London	14	21 gns.	Norwegian Fjords, Bergen, S'mpton
4	Lancastria (17,000 tons)	Cunard W. Star	Liverpool	13	£16	Casablanca, Las Palmas, Santa Cruz, Madeira, Liverpool.
4	Avoceta (3,500 tons)	Yeoward	Liverpool	22	23 gns.	Lisbon, Madeira, Las Palmas, Santa Cruz, La Palma, Orotava, Las Palmas, Liverpool.
4	Orion (24,000 tons)	Orient	Immingham	13	20 gns.	Balholm, Ulvik, Eidfjord, Stockholm, Copenhagen, Immingham.
4	Voltaire (13,248 tons)	Lamport & Holt	Southampton	13	16 gns.	Norwegian Fjords and Northern Capitals, Southampton.
4	City of Nagpur (10,138 tons)	Wilson	Hull	6	£6	Christiansand, Oslo, Hull.
4	Atlantis (16,000 tons)	Royal Mail	Southampton	12	19 gns.	Bologne, Oslo, Copenhagen, Stockholm, Zoppot, Kiel Canal, Holtenau, Brunsbuttel, Hamburg, London (Tilbury).
11	City of Nagpur (10,138 tons)	Wilson	Hull	6	£6	Christiansand, Oslo, Hull.
11	Vandyck (13,248 tons)	Lamport & Holt	Liverpool	12	15 gns.	Norwegian Fjords, Bergen, L'pool.
11	Orontes (20,000 tons)	Orient	Immingham	13	20 gns.	Zoppot, Helsingfors, Stockholm, Copenhagen, Immingham.
11	Aguila (3,500 tons)	Yeoward	Liverpool	22	23 gns.	Lisbon, Casablanca, Madeira, Santa Cruz, Orotava, Las Palmas, L'pool.
11	Strathaird (22,500 tons)	P. & O.	Southampton	13	£22 1st £12 t'rist	Barcelona, Bizerta, Malta, Palma, Southampton.
11	Arandora Star (15,000 tons)	Blue Star	Tilbury	20	30 gns.	Faroe Islands, Iceland, Spitzbergen, Norwegian Fjords, Bergen, Tilbury.
11	Cheshire (15,000 tons)	Bibby	London	7	8/10gns.	Hamburg, Antwerp, Liverpool.
11	Meteor (4,000 tons)	B. & N.	Newcastle	7	£12/10	Bergen, Norwegian Fjords, N'castle.
14	Gloucester Castle (8,006 tons)	Union Castle	London	10/11	12 gns. thro'out	Antwerp, Rotterdam, Hamburg, London.
15	Sarpedon (11,321 tons)	Blue Funnel	London	6	7 gns. thro'out	Glasgow, via N. and W. Coasts Scotland (with 2 days at Rotterdam).
16	Stella Polaris (6,000 tons)	B. & N.	Harwich	14	£27	Bergen, Norwegian Fjords, North Cape, Bergen, Harwich.
16	Tuscania (17,000 tons)	Anchor	Glasgow	14	15 gns.	Lisbon, Madeira, Teneriffe, Casablanca, Glasgow.
17	Calypso (4,000 tons)	Wilson	London	10	£10	Brunsbuttel, Holtenau, Copenhagen, Oslo, Christiansand, London.

List of cruises, 1936.

SUNSHINE CRUISES

T.S.S.
VOLTAIRE
and
VANDYCK

FIRST CLASS ONLY

Window or Porthole in every room.
ALL THE AMENITIES OF PLEASURE CRUISE SHIPS

Cruises by T.S.S. "Voltaire"

APRIL 9.—THURSDAY. (Easter Cruise)
From Southampton to Gibraltar, Casablanca
(for Rabat), Santa Cruz de la Palma,
Madeira (3 days stay), Lisbon .. *18 days from* **24 gns**

MAY 2.—SATURDAY
From Southampton to Casablanca, Dakar
(Senegal), Bathurst (Gambia), Santa
Cruz de la Palma, Madeira .. *21 days from* **28 gns**

MAY 30.—SATURDAY (Whitsun Cruise)
From Southampton to Gibraltar, Casablanca
(for Rabat) Santa Cruz de la Palma,
Madeira (3 days stay) Lisbon .. *18 days from* **24 gns**

JUNE 20.—SATURDAY
From Southampton to Cadiz, Palma
(Mallorca), Ceuta (for Tetuan),
Lisbon .. .. .. *13 days from* **16 gns**

Cruises by T.S.S. "Vandyck"

APRIL 9.—THURSDAY (Easter Cruise)
From Liverpool to Ceuta (for Tetuan),
Villefranche (for Monte Carlo, Nice,
etc.), Barcelona, Palma (Mallorca),
Lisbon .. .. .. *18 days from* **24 gns**

MAY 9.—SATURDAY.
From Liverpool to Vigo, Ceuta (for Tetuan),
Palma (Mallorca), Gibraltar .. *13 days from* **16 gns**

MAY 30.—SATURDAY (Whitsun Cruise)
From Liverpool to Gibraltar, Palma (Mallorca), Ceuta, Lisbon .. .. *13 days from* **16 gns**

JUNE 13.—SATURDAY
From Liverpool to Tangier, Casablanca
(for Rabat), Madeira, Lisbon .. *13 days from* **16 gns**

JUNE 27.—SATURDAY
From Liverpool to Norwegian Fjords and
Bergen .. .. .. *13 days from* **16 gns**

*Full programme of Cruises, 1936, to Riviera, Morocco,
Atlantic Isles, Norway, Northern Capitals, &c.*
can be obtained from

LAMPORT & HOLT LINE Ltd.
Royal Liver Building, LIVERPOOL.

Voltaire and
Vandyck cruises,
1936.

HENDERSON LINE

Regular Passenger Services

Gibraltar	-	£14 Return
Palma	-	£18 Return
Marseilles	-	£19 Return

also
EGYPT, SUDAN and BURMA

For full particulars apply

P. HENDERSON & CO.
Head Office:
95,
Bothwell Street,
GLASGOW, C.2.
or
48-50 St. Mary Axe
LONDON, E.C.3.
Royal Liver
Building,
LIVERPOOL.

ELDER DEMPSTER LINES

WINTER TOURS TO MADEIRA AND THE CANARY ISLANDS

AVAILABLE OCTOBER-APRIL

SPECIAL REDUCED RETURN FARES
FIRST SALOON   SECOND SALOON
£20-0-0   £15-0-0

TOURS TO WEST AFRICA

ELDER DEMPSTER LINES, LTD.
HEAD OFFICE : 30 WATER STREET,
Liverpool, 2.

TO AND FROM WEST AFRICA

N.Y.K. LINE

Fortnightly Cargo & Passenger Service from

MIDDLESBRO', ANTWERP, LONDON, GIBRALTAR, & MARSEILLES to CEYLON, STRAITS, CHINA & JAPAN.

REDUCED RETURN FARE
FIRST CLASS
LONDON TO JAPAN from **£128**

Monthly Cargo Service from
NEWPORT, SWANSEA, GLASGOW AND BIRKENHEAD TO STRAITS, CHINA AND JAPAN.

For Further Particulars apply :—

Nippon Yusen Kaisha,
88 LEADENHALL ST., LONDON, E.C.3.
Tel. AVENUE 8061 (7 lines).
India Buildings, Water Street, LIVERPOOL.
or Local Agents.

Royal Mail & Pacific Lines
TO SOUTH AMERICA

PASSENGER AND FREIGHT SERVICES
To BRAZIL, URUGUAY & ARGENTINA,
From Southampton, London and Liverpool.

Tours to Spain, Portugal, Madeira & Canary Islands

From LIVERPOOL to BERMUDA, BAHAMAS, HAVANA, PANAMA, PERU, CHILE.

Tours to Bermuda and Bahamas inclusive of Hotel.

ROYAL MAIL LINES, LTD.
THE PACIFIC STEAM NAVIGATION COMPANY.

London : America House, Cockspur Street, S.W.1., Royal Mail House, Leadenhall Street, E.C.3. Liverpool : Goree, Water Street. Glasgow, Birmingham, Southampton, Manchester, Cardiff or Local Agents.

CHARIVARI.—MAY 6, 1931.   xli

"ARANDORA STAR" CRUISES

MEDITERRANEAN

SPECIAL WHITSUN CRUISE
May 23rd — 16 days. Fare from 25 gns. Visiting Lisbon, Tangier, Casablanca, Las Palmas, Teneriffe, Madeira, Arosa Bay (for Santiago).

TO THE NORWEGIAN FJORDS
June 13th— 13 days. Fare from 20 gns. To Ulvik, Eidfjord, Trondhjem, Aandalsnaes, Molde, Oie, Hellesylt, Merok, Olden, Loen, Balholm, Gudvangen, Bergen.

TO THE NORWEGIAN FJORDS & NORTHERN CAPITALS
To Balholm, Gudvangen, Bergen, Eidfjord, Ulvik, Oslo, Arendal, Christiansand, Copenhagen, Gothenburg. June 27. From 20 gns.

& NORWAY

THE world's most bracing, most enchanting Holiday is a Blue Star Cruise, with the highest standard of comfort and service ever set in the proud traditions of the sea. No vessel afloat can approach the "Arandora Star" for sheer charm, luxury and comfort.

For full particulars of these and other cruises apply to

THE BLUE STAR LINE

3, Lower Regent Street, London, S.W.1. (Gerrard 5671). Liverpool, 10, Water Street, and Principal Tourist Agents.

Choose your Cruise
FROM THESE GLORIOUS 1938 ATTRACTIONS ON THE NEW

ARANDORA STAR

The World's most delightful Cruising Liner
Only one sitting for meals

THE quiet luxurious comfort of the new Public Rooms, the Cuisine, Service, ample Games Decks, the grand Ballroom, restful silent Sun Deck, make Arandora Star Cruises events that remain happy memories throughout one's life.

APRIL 14 Algiers, Kotor, Dubrovnik, Split, Abbazia, Venice, Brioni, Corfu, Villefranche for Nice and Monte Carlo.   *13 DAYS from 48 GNS.*

MAY 14 Algiers, Rapallo, Naples (for Pompeii, Amalfi, etc.), Messina, Malta, Bizerta (for Tunis)   *18 DAYS from 32 GNS.*

JUNE 3 Annual Birthday Cruise to Villefranche (for Nice and Monte Carlo), Naples (for Pompeii, etc.), Kotor (Cattaro), Dubrovnik (Ragusa), Athens, Philippeville (for Constantine), Lisbon (for Escoril).   *22 DAYS from 37 GNS.*

JUNE 25 Hamburg, Brunsbuttel, Holtenau, Kiel, Stockholm, Visby, Zoppot (for Danzig), Copenhagen   *13 DAYS from 22 GNS.*

JULY 9 Trangisvaag, Reykjavik, Jan Mayen Isle, Magdalen Bay, The Great Ice Barrier, (only 590 miles from North Pole yet warm as Springtime), Cross Bay, King's Bay, Smeren Bay, Advent Bay, Green Harbour, Bear Island, North Cape, Hammerfest, Lyngen, Tromso, Trondheim, Merok, Olden, Loen, Aardal, Laerdal, Bergen.   *20 DAYS from 34 GNS.*

JULY 30 Bergen, Fåardalsnaes, Molde, Merok, Olden, Loen, Copenhagen, Bornholm, Kiel, Holtenau, Brunsbuttel, Hamburg.   *13 DAYS from 22 GNS.*

AUGUST 13 Oslo, Copenhagen, Visby, Stockholm, Helsingfors, Pillau, Zoppot (for Danzig), Bornholm, Travemunde (for Lubeck), Kiel, Holtenau, Brunsbuttel.   *19 DAYS from 33 GNS.*

SEPT. 2 Villefranche (for Nice and Monte Carlo), Naples (for Pompeii, etc.), Kotor (Cattaro), Dubrovnik (Ragusa), Athens, Philippeville (for Constantine), Lisbon (for Escoril).   *21 DAYS from 40 GNS.*

SEPT. 24 Malta, Athens, Gallipoli—Salvo Bay, Anzac Bay, Cape Helles, Dardanelles (Chanak), Istanbul, Rhodes, Lanarka, Haifa, (for Nazareth), Jaffa (for Jerusalem), Port Said (for Cairo), Alexandria, Palermo.   *28 DAYS from 50 GNS.*

OCT. 22 Midsummer in Autumn Cruise, Lisbon (for Estoril), Madeira, Dakar, Freetown, Las Palmas, Safi (for Marrakesh).   *21 DAYS from 36 GNS.*

DEC. 21 Xmas and New Year Sunshine Cruise to West Africa, Equator and Atlantic Islands.   *22 DAYS from 43 GNS.*

BLUE STAR LINE

3, Lower Regent Street, S.W.1   'Phone : Whitehall 2266
Liverpool, Birmingham, Manchester or Travel Agents

Above left: 1936 adverts for Henderson Line, Elder Dempster, NYK Line and Royal Mail and Pacific Lines to South America.

Above middle and right: 1935 adverts for *Arandora Star* cruises.

Arandora Star was built as *Arandora* in 1927 for the Blue Star Line and was converted to a cruise liner by Fairfield Ship Building & Engineering Company two years later. Her first cruise was from Immingham to Norway and she was later based at Southampton. She was given a white hull with a red band in 1931 and a Vent-Axia ventilation system was installed in 1938. During the Second World War she was initially used as a test ship for net defences and later as a troopship. On 3 July 1940 she was torpedoed by U-47 and sank in just over an hour with a loss of 805 lives.

Left: *Queen Mary* sports deck.

Below: *Queen Mary* cabin-class lounge.

Queen Mary prepares to sail from Southampton.

Queen Mary.

Queen Mary cabin-class restaurant.

Queen Mary bridge.

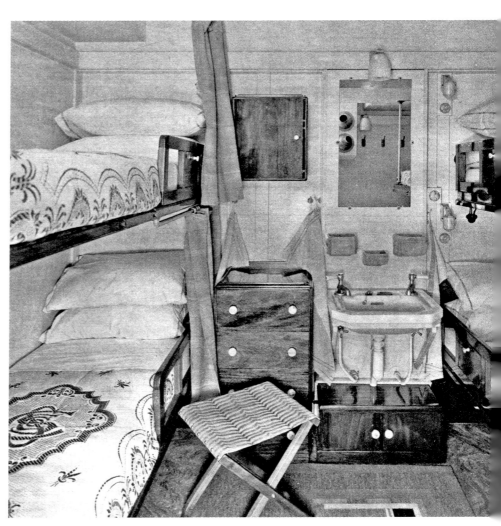

Above: Queen Mary first-class stateroom.

Right: Queen Mary third-class bedroom.

Above and right: Queen Mary list of crew.

Right: Queen Elizabeth list of crew.

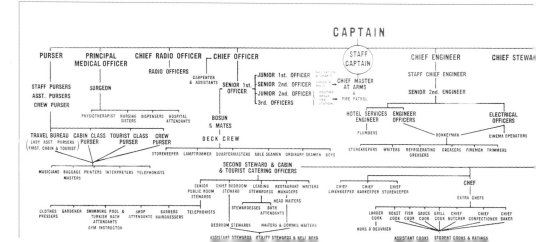

"Caledonia" CRUISES
ITINERARIES

CRUISE 1
14th-28th JULY
14 Days from 16 gns.

PORT	MILES	ARRIVE	DEPART	Hrs. Stay
GLASGOW	—	—	7.30 p.m. Fri. 14th July	—
Lisbon	1,097	8 a.m. Tues. 18th July	2 a.m. Wed. 19th July	18
Madeira	528	1 p.m. Thur. 20th July	5 p.m. Fri. 21st July	28
Casablanca	472	8 a.m. Sun. 23rd July	7 p.m. Sun. 23rd July	11
Gibraltar	190	10 a.m. Mon. 24th July	6 p.m. Mon. 24th July	8
GLASGOW	1,373	9.30 p.m. Fri. 28th July	—	—

CRUISE 2
29th JULY-7th AUGUST
8 Days from 10 gns.

PORT	MILES	ARRIVE	DEPART	Hrs. Stay
GLASGOW	—	—	9 p.m. Sat. 29th July	—
Oslo	890	1 p.m. Tues. 1st Aug.	8 a.m. Wed. 2nd Aug.	19
Copenhagen	272	8 a.m. Thur. 3rd Aug.	6 a.m. Fri. 4th Aug.	22
GLASGOW	977	8 a.m. Mon. 7th Aug.	—	—

CRUISE 3
11th-29th AUGUST
17 Days from 19 gns.

PORT	MILES	ARRIVE	DEPART	Hrs. Stay
GLASGOW	—	—	7 p.m. Fri. 11th Aug.	—
Belfast	112	8 a.m. Sat. 12th Aug.	9 a.m. Sat. 12th Aug.	1
Dublin	100	4 p.m. Sat. 12th Aug.	5 p.m. Sat. 12th Aug.	1
Lisbon	917	8 a.m. Tues. 15th Aug.	3 a.m. Wed. 16th Aug.	19
Monte Carlo	1,129	8 a.m. Sat. 19th Aug.	2 a.m. Sun. 20th Aug.	18
Naples	365	7 a.m. Mon. 21st Aug.	2 a.m. Tues. 22nd Aug.	19
Algiers	607	5 p.m. Wed. 23rd Aug.	Noon Thur. 24th Aug.	19
Dublin	1,632	10 p.m. Mon. 28th Aug.	11 p.m. Mon. 28th Aug.	1
Belfast	100	5.30 a.m. Tues. 29th Aug.	6 a.m. Tues. 29th Aug.	½
GLASGOW	112	2 p.m. Tues. 29th Aug.	—	—

Shore Excursions : See separate booklet for rates and particulars.

Above: Anchor Line's *Circassia* in the River Mersey. She was built in 1937 for the company's service from Glasgow and Liverpool to Bombay. She operated as an Armed Merchant Cruiser and troopship from 1940 to 1942 and was rebuilt as a Landing Ship Infantry in 1943. Returned to service in 1947, she made Anchor Line's final passenger sailing in 1966 and was broken up at Alicante later that year.

Left: Anchor Line's 1939 *Caledonia* cruise itineraries.

Typical scenes aboard a 1930s cruise ship.

Above: A number of smaller vessels operated cruises around the coast of Britain in the twentieth century. *Queen of the South* is seen here on a cruise in the Thames.

Right: Clyde paddle steamer.

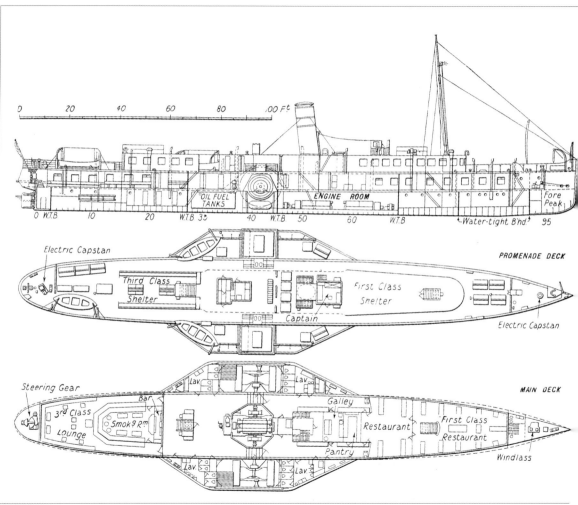

Paddle steamer *Sandown* off the Isle of Wight.

Consol at Lulworth.

Waverley on the River Clyde.

Jeanie Deans also on the Clyde.

Medway Queen.

Britannia at Bristol.

Above: Bristol Queen.

Right: Ravenswood.

Left: *Orion* on a rare visit to the River Mersey. She was built by Vickers Armstrong at Barrow-in-Furness in 1935 for the Orient Lines Australian service. *Orion* spent most of the Second World War on trooping duties, resuming the Australian service in 1947. In 1954 she was operating on the Sydney–Auckland–Vancouver–San Francisco route, and in 1963 she was used as a hotel ship at Hamburg before being broken up in Belgium.

Below left and right: Passengers enjoy a cruise on the Orient Line *Oronsay*.

P&O's *Stratheden* was built at Barrow in 1937. She operated as a troopship during the Second World War, returning to service in 1947. In 1950 she was chartered to the Cunard Line and made four round voyages to New York. In 1963 she was chartered to the Travel Savings Association to undertake a series of cruises for that organisation. The following year she was sold to John S. Latsis and renamed *Henrietta Latsis*, becoming *Marianna Latsis* two years later. She was broken up in 1969.

Strathmore was completed in 1935 for the Australian service. She operated as a troopship from 1939 to 1945, taking her first post war voyage in October 1949. She was also sold to John S. Latsis and renamed *Marianna Latsis* in 1963 and *Henrietta Latsis* three years later. She was broken up in 1969.

ARANDORA STAR
MEDITERRANEAN HOLIDAY CRUISES

1939

Menu

BREAKFAST

Chilled Grape Fruit   Fresh Orange Juice
Oranges   Apples   Bananas
Stewed Prunes, Figs and Apricots
Quaker Oats   Oatmeal Porridge   Hominy
Post Toasties   Force   Shredded Wheat   Kellogg's Bran
Puffed Rice   Grape Nuts   Creamed Barley   Corn Flakes
Buckwheat Cakes and Maple Syrup
Smoked London Haddock   Fried Fresh Fish with Lemon
Hashed Poultry à la King
Fried, Mashed and Saute Potatoes

To Order and from the Grill :
Eggs : Fried, Turned, Boiled, Scrambled, Poached
Omelets : Plain, Ham, Parsley, Cheese, Tomato
Danish Breakfast Bacon   Cumberland Ham
Calves' Liver   Tomatoes   Minute Steaks

Cold Sideboard :
York Ham   Ox-Tongue   Leicester Pie
Boar's Head   Oxford Brawn
Anchovy and Bloater Paste
Radishes, Spring Onions

White and Graham Rolls   Baton   Coburg   Twin Rolls
French Crescents   Hovis Bread   Pulled Bread
Energen Bread   Ryvita Bread   Toast   Turog Bread
Hot Cream Scones   Sultana Buns   Sally Lunns
Conserves : Marmalade, Guava Jelly, Preserved Ginger,
Assorted Jams, Honey in Comb

Tea   Coffee   Cocoa   Iced Tea   Iced Coffee

Cruising Liner "ARANDORA STAR,"
Spitzbergen Cruise—at Immingham—July 31st, 1931

The Blue Star Line's *Arandora Star* was one of the most popular of the 1930s cruise ships. She undertook many cruises all over the world, and was famously painted in an all-over white livery. Immingham was a popular departure point on the East Coast for cruises to the Baltic, Norway, Iceland and Spitzbergen.

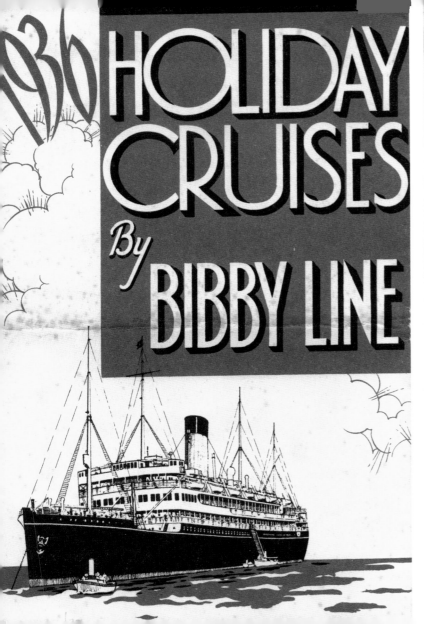

Opposite: Coastal and short sea ships were used for cruising too, and as the Finland Line stated, often off the beaten track. Many lines, such as McCallum, Orme in Scotland and Coast Lines, based in LIverpool, as well as the Clyde Shipping Co. and Aberdeen Steam Navigation Co. operated coastal cruises.

Bibby Line ships were mainly used for trooping. As the need declined in the 1930s, the ships were sent cruising instead.

Come to FINLAND

An ideal holiday-off the beaten track.
CRUISES in the BALTIC
by the FINLAND LINE of MAIL STEAMERS
FROM HULL

BOOKING AGENTS   BROOK FLOWERS & Co. LTD.

HOLIDAYS

CLYDE
SHIPPING
COMPANY
LIMITED

Right and opposite page: The Canadian Pacific liners *Empress of Scotland* and *Empress of France. Empress of Scotland* was built in 1930 as *Empress of Japan* and sailed on her maiden voyage from Liverpool to Quebec and back to Southampton. She then sailed from Southampton on 12 June to Suez, Hong Kong, Yokohama and Vancouver. In 1942, when acting as a troopship, she was renamed *Empress of Scotland* and arrived at Liverpool on 3 May 1948 to be decommissioned and return to commercial duties on the Liverpool–Canada service. She was sold to Hamburg Atlantic Line in 1958 and renamed *Hanseatic.* However, on 7 September 1966 she caught fire at New York and was later broken up at Hamburg. *Empress of France* was originally named *Duchess of Bedford* and was built by John Brown at Glasgow in 1928. She operated as a troopship during the Second World War and was originally to be renamed *Empress of India.* However, she emerged from her refit in 1947 as *Empress of France.* She left Liverpool on 19 December 1960 to be broken up.

THE BLUE FUNNEL LINE

FIRST CLASS PASSENGERS ONLY.

CRUISES DOWN THE WESTERN ISLES

LONDON TO GLASGOW via the NORTH AND WEST COASTS OF SCOTLAND
With two days in HOLLAND Six days **7 gns.**
Sailing 21 Apr. 19 May. 20 June 15 July.
12 Aug. 9 Sept. 6 Oct.
In vessels over 10,000 tons.

Summer Return Fares to the Canary Islands ... ... £17.
MAY TO SEPTEMBER.

INCLUSIVE TOURS TO CAIRO
22 DAYS AFLOAT   3/4 DAYS IN EGYPT   £40
Sailing 13 June. 11 July. 8 Aug. 5 Sept.

For further particulars apply—
INDIA BUILDINGS, LIVERPOOL
8, Billiter Square, 101, Leadenhall Street, London
69, Buchanan Street, 80, Buchanan Street, Glasgow

THE BLUE FUNNEL LINE

SEA VOYAGES

CRUISES DOWN THE WESTERN ISLES
London to Glasgow via the North and West Coasts of Scotland
with two days in Holland
SIX DAYS—7 Gns.———In vessels over 10,000 tons

INCLUSIVE SUMMER HOLIDAY TOUR TO SOUTH AFRICA
Sailing 27th July———Arriving home 10th September
40 DAYS AFLOAT — 5 DAYS IN CAPETOWN—£65

INCLUSIVE TOURS TO CAIRO
Vessel—Rail—Hotel—£40

ALFRED HOLT & CO., LIVERPOOL
OR LOCAL AGENTS

Sarpedon berthing at Liverpool landing stage. She was built by Cammell Laird at Birkenhead in 1923 as the first of a class of four ships to accommodate 155 first-class passengers and a crew of eighty. The passengers were accommodated in one-, two- and three-berth rooms. The saloon was in the fore end of the centrecastle and was the full breadth of the ship, with pantries and galleys abaft of it. A lounge, smoking room and veranda café were provided on the promenade deck and a children's playground on the bridge deck. She survived the Second World War and took the first post-war sailing from Liverpool to Brisbane with forty-eight passengers. She was broken up at Newport in 1953.

The Fares shown are in operation as follows:

To and from GIBRALTAR
    MARSEILLES   } Throughout the Year.
    & NAPLES

To PORT SAID   ... From " KASHIMA MARU " 3rd April up to
    and including the " KASHIMA MARU "
    21st August.

From PORT SAID   ... From " TERUKUNI MARU " 15th May up
    to the end of December.

Passengers taking return tickets to Port Said cannot return prior to 15th May.

Similarly, passengers taking return tickets from Port Said must return not later than by the " KASHIMA MARU " from London 21st August, Marseilles 28th August, Naples 30th August.

The following charges are payable by passengers and should be remitted in addition to the passage money:—

NAPLES PORT AND BAGGAGE PORTERAGE TAXES.
The following Taxes are levied by the Italian authorities on passengers embarking or disembarking at Naples:—

	1st Class.	2nd Class.
From London to Naples - - -	lires 45	lires 20
,, Gibraltar to Naples - -	,, 19	,, 11
,, Marseilles to Naples - -	,, 19	,, 11
,, Naples to Port Said - -	,, 26	,, 18

Special Return First Class Fares

Operative Throughout the Year

From

LONDON

To

SINGAPORE	from	£112
HONGKONG	,,	123
SHANGHAI		128
JAPAN	,,	128

Availability 150 Days.   Stop over allowed at any Port of Call.

———————

Reduced Around-the-World Fares.

By N.Y.K. from London, to Gibraltar, Marseilles, Naples, Port Said, Colombo, Singapore, Hong Kong, Shanghai, Kobe and Yokohama; thence via Honolulu to San Francisco or to Vancouver and Seattle. Choice of any direct railway route from Port of Landing to any North American or Canadian Atlantic Coast Port, thence to European Port by any Atlantic Line. Fares from £91 providing second and tourist class accommodation, to £166 providing first class accommodation throughout.

1936 NYK Line Mediterranean tours from London to Gibraltar, Marseilles, Naples and Port Said.

Opposite page: Another NYK brochure, this time from 1938.

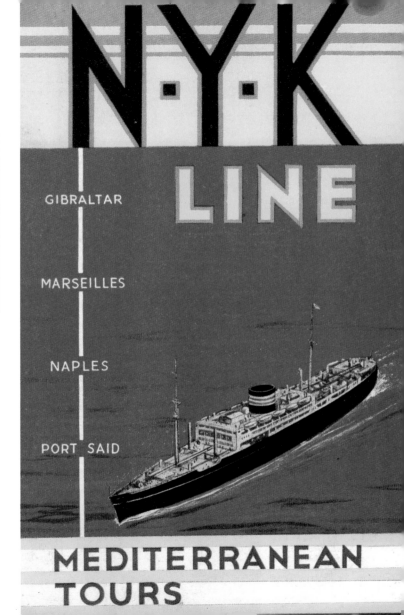

Coast Lines operated cruises around the coast of the British Isles and Ireland with, from top to bottom, *Pacific Coast*, *Gloucester Coast* and *Ocean Coast*.

CALCUTTA-FAR EAST SERVICE

 *presents*

SANGOLA and SANTHIA

BRITISH INDIA STEAM NAVIGATION COMPANY LIMITED

The British India Line passenger vessels *Sangola* and *Santhia* operated a service between Calcutta and the Far East. The brochure described the B-I plan thus: 'The British India tradition of fast, comfortable spacious ocean travel is fully upheld by the *Sangola* and *Santhia*. The first of these motor ships is of 8,600 gross tons, while the second is of 8,908 tons. Both operate direct services between Calcutta, Rangoon, Malaya, Hong Kong and Japan. They provide the ideal opportunity for a comfortable holiday at sea and they offer an Express Cargo Service which enables shippers of urgent cargoes to save time and money. These ships implement the British India plan to maintain the kind of service that has been operated proudly in the East for over a century.'

Mauretania was built by Cammell Laird at Birkenhead in 1939. Following a very short period on the North Atlantic crossings she was converted to a troopship in 1940 for war service, arriving back in Liverpool on 2 August 1946 after completing 48 trooping voyages and carrying over 355,000 troops. She returned to service on 26 April the following year and cruised out of New York in the winter months. In September 1962 she was painted green for cruising and the following year was placed on the New York–Cannes–Genoa–Naples route. However, this service did not prove successful or profitable and she was sold to be broken up at Inverkeithing in 1965.

THE NORTH OF SCOTLAND ORKNEY & SHETLAND STEAM NAVIGATION COY

ST MAGNUS HOTEL, HILLSWICK, SHETLAND.

Opened 1900, under the Company's management, affords excellent accommodation for visitors at moderate rates. There is good and extensive loch and sea fishing in the neighbourhood. The coast scenery is grand. Tudor in his "Orkney and Shetland," published in 1883, page 533, says:—"When, as must come sooner or later, proper accommodation is provided throughout the length and breadth of Shetland for travellers in search of the beautiful, who will flock northwards, there will be no spot in all Hjaltland which in its manifold attractions will be so popular as 'Grey Hillswick.'" Apply to the Manageress of the Hotel, Hillswick.

S.S. "ST NINIAN"